About the Author

Mohannad Halaby (M.H.) believes that the inner struggles of a person are the secrets that shape an individual's character. He believes in the love of God being beneficial to the human self: "What good will it be for someone to gain the whole world, yet forfeit their Soul" (Matthew 16: 26)

M. H. was afraid of those words. His confusion wasn't of losing himself, but from the fear of not abiding by the Lord's words at times. M.H. was honest with his needs.

He achieved an incredible accomplishment of writing his first book within only twenty one days. After that M.H. stated,

"Man can achieve phenomenal and unique feats if he or she intended to be truthful with himself or herself. However, if they verily counted on God, they will indeed perform unbelievable miracles."

Acknowledgments

I would like to thank all with thanks to my family and especially my brothers, Tawfik Halaby, Faisal Halaby as also Rawad Zeineddine, Nabil Imad, Wissam Jaramany. Bashir Kashkash, & my cousins, Wajdi Saleh Azzam, Bassam Barakat & Bachir Azzam, and all other true brothers and sisters who encouraged me to show this book to the world. I would also like to thank Proudly, I want to thank Austin Macauley Publishers, including all its respectful departments, who acted truly as my family, and accompanied me throughout the publishing process to successfully publish this book.

Dedications

With my greatest respects, I dedicate this book for the Soul of my Supporter and Big brother, Dr. Sami Makarem who died on the 21st of August 2012.

As I also dedicate this book for the Soul of my dear Raed Raydan who died in May 5th 2009

Finally, this book is dedicated to every reader who is passionate to seek the truth.

Mohannad Halaby

Twenty One Days

AUSTIN MACAULEY
PUBLISHERS LTD.

A CIP catalogue record for this title is available from the British Library.

ISBN 9781785543104 (Paperback)
ISBN 9781785543111 (Hardback)

www.austinmacauley.com

First Published (2015)
Austin Macauley Publishers Ltd.
25 Canada Square
Canary Wharf
London
E14 5LQ

Printed and bound in Great Britain

Introduction

"I write life, and others read it" was something I once wrote for my beloved ones as a challenge for death after passing my worst times ever. Surely the word 'others' wasn't meant for all of the public, but it was dedicated to the special ones who occupied a big part of my life and let my writing explain my inner stories, in which they became my heroes.

I used to write, but now not so much. It was done only through times when I was in love.

Someone also used to say:
"We are always enemies of the unknown."
That saying impressed me to a level that gave me the passion to prove its meaning through my first book, which will show a little of my inner stories.

Well, this book could be better understood if the reader compares it with the unique coincidences mentioned later.
The first one I remember, happened when the girl I loved called and said that she was reminded of me while listening to a special song playing on the radio. This was very unusual, as she normally never tuned in. I answered with a true smile, and told her that I was the one who requested the song from the radio operator accidently.
I can remember the second coincidence well, and it happened every morning. I saw a smiley face followed by the French word 'Bonjour' drawn on my action plan by a special colleague. My first reaction was to smile broadly at my students, but deeply it was meant for her - the girl who

was surely smiling back at me in the same way that I smile every time I think about this fond memory.

Sitting in a peaceful place surrounded by lovely trees, feeling the breeze touching my hands, I held my notebook open on a special date and passed over my greatest recollections to weave the story of my heart and my mind combined together.

"In the name of the Lord, I start..."

Chapter 1

"Reflections of My Life."

My best memories are made of both hard and good times, and began at the time I stood on the balcony of my home, watching the flying pigeons and noticing a letter M in their arrangement, with a lovely white pigeon showing clearly.

I was thinking about my problems that were a result of a near future decision, coming from painful past events through which had no solution at that present time.

Running away or hiding was never my way in facing life, traveling was the only way to start again. This could help in reconstructing myself from a belief which had nothing except a strong love.

I was never impressed by any love story like the one that I was living with my beloved girl.

It was a dream coming true in every day we both lived.

It was lighting my destiny with peace and filled me with happiness. At times my beloved girl and I faced problems with our united heart against the surroundings, against time, against anything that tried to affect our relationship.

"Till death do us part, I will continue on loving you", was what I once wrote for a girl who thought of me as I did, and dreamed about me as her future husband; likewise I always dreamt of her as a future wife and a mother of my children.

That girl sacrificed her life, her decisions, her studies, society, family and everything just to be with me.

We lived a life which all of our society admitted that no couple had before; in love, in mind and in soul.

It was a relationship of pure feelings, innocent love and honest words that never lied.

"Being truthful is above everything", was our first principle, because lies destroy love. Consequently, trust will be gone and our minds will be slaves to those who made us liars. So no one was allowed to intrude in our problems, even if it was for the sake of helping us.

"I want to understand you alone as you want to do with me."

"It's our word and our responsibility."

"It's you and I who decide the duration of our relation's life."

"Together in sadness and happiness", we both agreed.

Those were some of the foundations that we used to heal and cure any problem we faced through that relationship.

Unity was all that we aimed at. She left her university in the USA after she finished the first year in American Law with a full scholarship and made the decision to come back to learn in my country at my university after we fell in love during her summer vacation.

All her relatives, friends, and even her parents saw that she became irresponsible and reckless after she made her decision to leave everything for a sentimental reason.

But that girl was totally convinced by her steps and arrangements and chose to start all over again with Political Sciences which was the only choice since she had a background of Law studies.

She sacrificed her life with confidence, just to build a future made of pure love with a truthful partner who loved and wanted her for her character and spontaneity, and not for any other reason.

I was still nineteen when I visited her parents alone. I informed them that their daughter had become my fiancé and that we were now engaged.

My parents were surprised when I came back home and told them that I had proposed to a girl called Robina.

"I'm in total charge of my words and I'm convinced of what I'm doing, father. This girl is now my responsibility." I said.

"Well, what do you think of sending us a marriage card when you want to marry." My father answered and laughed with my mother at my reckless acts that made them feel as if they were not in charge of anything. "Her parents were also astonished like you, father, and considered it a daring step. They thought that as if I was still young for marriage, but they respected my words because they really felt that I was being truthful. In the end, I respect you both, but that feeling was killing me inside. I couldn't sleep last night, just waiting to confess my feelings to her family. I can't be fake dad, and pretend that I'm only a friend. I want to visit her house regularly".

I continued, "I know this is disrespectful for you as my parents to enter another home without you, but I had truthful intentions. I love her to death, as she does me. I saw myself able of being her husband later in life. So without hesitation to delay this step, I went as I always do in everything I believe in, dad. I think you and mother understand me more than anyone else in this world."

Dad replied, "Son, we don't care about protocols when we see our little man happy, just continue like that and do whatever you love and whatever you see right. We love you too, as we trust in you and we are very proud of having such a sweet responsible truthful son like you."

My mother smiled as if she was in heaven. She didn't say a word. But stood up to interrupt my father's sweet words by a kiss on my head.

I hugged them both and laughed with them on my crazy funny behaviour.

Since then, I started visiting my girl's home as one of her family members. It was the best thing I've ever done.

"That's me, and I don't care about my age or the traditions as much as being truthful. I love you and if God wills, you will be my future wife and the mother of my children," I said later to Robina.

"Don't say if God wills, because surely God wanted us together. We are one, and as you always say,

'Till death do us part'." was her reply; full of fear of the possible obstacles which might separate us.

The University used to have regional activities for the African countries. It organized a one-week trip for university students only.

We went there after the consent of both parents. It was after the best days, our relationship experienced true affection and passion.

It was an educational trip to learn about new cultures and to show how poor countries could progress by exchanging knowledge about human resources.

We got to know many people who were able to benefit instead of just being given food.

It was a special project our university organized in order to connect with other civilizations via learning methodology.

It was an amazing experience we had at a young age, however an important point was overlooked - the timing of the trip.

It was the beginning of a political conflict in the African country. Within days the revolution escalated to a serious up-rising against the government. Unfortunately our residence was near that hot spot.

We risked our lives as we tried to escape when snipers were shooting from different roofs in the region.

I picked up my beloved girl and her friends to her apartment located beside the university and made my best to secure their escape away from that remote region which was controlled by the local rebels.

The army was unable to control the situation. I went down and asked the soldiers three times to let me take the girls away, but at every time they asked me to go back to safety until the area was clear enough to run away.

However, I noticed that the revolt was getting worse. The gunmen showed up in their hundreds as the snipers continued on shooting them.

The situation became totally dangerous. Two people were killed before our eyes.

It was not an ordinary accident. It was a start of a civil war and we got trapped in the battle field with only bare hands- nothing to protect my girl, her friends and myself. I spoke with the soldiers for the fourth time to allow me to make a way out by myself.

They didn't agree and told me to go back, but this time I refused and shouted at them. Then, angrily, I told the officer "I will take the responsibility to move the girls to safety before city roads get fully blocked."

I asked the girls to take each other's hands, I caught my sweetheart and carefully darted out and struggled to make a way through the wild battle.

I had the power of thousand men to protect Robina from any harm even if I had to put my life on the line.

In less than 30 minutes, we ran all the way to a bus station that had the last two buses loaded before the city closed.

The people on the two buses had no weapons. I asked the drivers,

"How can you go on with no arms? But they said, "God will save us."

My sweetheart asked me to stay in the bus that was about to move, but I refused and said,

"If you really love me, stay silent."

I told the driver to wait ten more minutes for me and I ran to grab any kind of weapon from the area. Luckily, I found a big knife from a butcher which was closing.

At that critical time, anything would do even a knife. I hurried back and asked the driver to move quickly.

The two bus drivers moved with wide smiles on their faces that showed a big thanks for my little help in securing the short run away from this foreign country. We went through different and dangerous regions. All the passengers from men and women were silent but feeling safe while they stared at me. I was fully alert and my senses were drawn to the slightest suspicion. I held Robina's arm with one hand to reassure her, and the knife in the other. God saved us that horrible day. As soon as we cleared the hot zone to the airport we immediately travelled directly to our country.

We made it together through this difficult time. It was a test of my readiness to defend my sweetheart at any cost. I cared less for anything I owned or my future investments as much as I cared for her well-being. That is why her family was at ease when she was with me.

Her parents sensed how close she became to my family. My parents loved her and could see we were in perfect harmony, united in one soul in two different bodies.

For four years we met daily, morning and evening, and on every vacation and holiday. We matched our schedules to see each other rather than learning. We kept an eye on each other wherever she was- in her classes or in the campus. I was so protective that I couldn't help but trace her footsteps. I showed my love to her obviously to all people to in a way to keep anyone envious away and to protect her from the guys who might desire her. We engraved our initials on a tree in the middle of the campus to make it everlasting. All the security guards in the university were my friends; I asked them to give Robina more priority to enter as VIP_which means to come in without being checked.

I could eat well, get sufficient sleep, and study hard only when I knew she was safe and secure.

In fact, she became my sister, my intimate friend, my daughter, and my darling. Simply, she was my everything.

Being under one roof was the only missing part to a fruitful marriage. Nevertheless, time was not a hindrance between us; I used to call her anytime!

"Its 2:30 am, are you alright?" She asked.

"Are you awake enough to listen?" I replied.

"Yes, honey I'm all ears," She repeated.

"I love you Robina and I'm impatient to wait for tomorrow to express my feelings. If you think I'm crazy, please, don't forget that you are literally my life with every breath I take and every step I make."

In a similar fashion, our beautiful days and romantic nights went by but forever recorded in letters and gifts well-chosen to reveal our affections and sentiments.

We waited for the celebrations which happened at the university workshop days. We never missed any birthday for any of our friends. Not because we were interested in their birthdays, but because we wanted to sit with each other and thank them for giving us the chance to meet in those events.

All people loved summer vacations since childhood, but we didn't. We were of the few students who registered for summer courses just to be around each other.

The longest vacation given was maximum 25 days which was the duration between the spring and summer semester.

Surely those 25 days couldn't go by without sitting with each other. I registered for elective courses that were shared by all departments.

But, first, I made sure that the doctors who taught the courses were all females or aged professors who became later my best friends.

I interfered and changed her other courses many times, but surely with her permission, and under the reason of:

"I know that Doctor well, and I know that he is going to be a source of trouble to me with his smiles to you."

Those summer courses were the best parts of the whole year. They gave me the chance to enjoy learning on the same desk with my beloved girl rather than waiting till the break times.

We waited for those classes and talked secretly as kids. We hid behind other students' heads to say secretly what we felt for each other, then wrote on both copybooks words that were never meant to be forgotten.

But overall, I couldn't forget our eyes which bore all the language that spoke everything.

Surely my senses were tuned to detect perfectly anyone who dared to look at her.

Once, while we first entered an elective course, we sat on a high row with a huge number of students who went on saying their names in order from upper to lower rows. The class was peaceful, but started to change when the name order arrived to the first row.

A student who looked a perfect trouble maker, said his full name to show that he was the son of a strong influential Minister who used to threaten others with his high political power.

In the middle of the session, Robina asked the Doctor a question, but that student turned as if he wanted to answer showing that he was impressed by her curiosity with an evil smile.

The Doctor got afraid and asked her to repeat what he really heard in order to avoid any participation and to make all focus on his answer only.

But directly and without thinking, I asked her to stop the repeated question and I asked that student loudly and sarcastically, "Look at me dear, maybe I can help you to answer the question."

He looked at all the students, and then at me angrily, without expecting anyone to face him.

But I repeated with a louder voice

"I'm asking you kid"

He looked down, stood up, turned and moved outside.

But I stood up too and made my way down, then headed down directly after him.

The doctor and all others were watching silently. I went down and opened the door looking after him.

He went far, but was standing outside calling somebody and stared at me as if waiting for me to follow him.

I understood well that I was in big trouble with a company of troublemakers. This fear was confirmed when I saw three guys I used to know moving outside the class to stare at me, they were followers of that Minister's son.

They were preparing for a fight outside. I called my close friends including my brother and asked them to come immediately to the university.

I went back and opened the door of the class and asked Robina to move down, without any permission from the frightened doctor.

I accompanied her to the emergency backdoors. She asked me to run away from the area because all the students indoors were saying that something bad was going to happen for me from that influential troublemaker.

I was listening to her and watching around for someone new on our way to her apartment.

She exclaimed, "Promise me you will run away. Please honey, I don't want anything to happen for you. I was the reason, and I will do anything to solve what I've done."

She was begging me to hide. "You can solve everything by staying in your apartment till I call you back baby," was my answer after I felt secure I had shut her apartment door and heard her lock it.

I called some of the university guards and asked them about the number of troublemakers who were on the university's main gate.

They asked me to stay away because their number was increasing quickly- even more than the university's security guards who were afraid of what was going to happen.

I waited for ten more minutes on the stairs until I heard my brother calling. He said that he and many of his friends were standing by my sweetheart's apartment. They were waiting for me to go back to face the other troublemakers at the main gate of the university.

I came down and moved to the university's main gate and looked for the Minister's son to check if he still wants to fight, being backed up by his friends. In contrast my friends followed me as fearless brothers unlike his father's followers.

The security watched and waited for the fight to start. I came to the middle of the outer entrance and took my fighting position, then my brother asked me loudly,

"Do you want to start anything bro? We came here for you and to beat the hell out of anyone who messes with you."

My friends readied themselves too and heard me answer.

"Brothers, we never attack and harm anyone except when we are threatened, and till now I didn't see anyone bold enough to confront me."

The Minister's Son realized that I was able to face him with a matching power.

He looked at his guys and slowly moved outside the campus away from the university, as if not beaten but avoiding a fight with honour.

For two more weeks, all the university students were watching my friends coming into the university regardless of the cost of any trouble, just to make sure that my sweetheart and I were safe.

Later, that Minister's son quit the course to avoid any contact with someone who had no fear of all his powers and showed that he would meet his doom if he even smiled to my darling.

Chapter 2

"Painful Memories"

The thought of deserting that girl was similar to abandoning my brother, sister or any of my family in the battle field.

She felt the same of course.

But a destructive accident happened, and unfortunately, the idea of breaking apart appeared to be the only solution for us.

"I don't know why I feel that something is going to happen to our relationship," was what I said to Robina from the hospital after an accident I had on my motorcycle as a consequence of my absent-mindedness.

"I prefer to kill myself instead of living a day away from you", was her interruption for my depressed words when she called me from another hospital after having a breakdown after my accident.

Then she repeated, "I don't know how you became so blind. Can't you notice that we are still one?"

There was a long pause.

Then I told her that I need to be on my own while knowing that rest was far away.

"Till death do us part." echoed deep inside as if to remind me not to end my life with a merciless bullet to relieve me from the agony.

I cried and begged God for help. That girl was my life; leaving her was a choice I never expected.

Leaving Robina was done only on one condition; that I leave myself to destiny, to the darkness, to my emotional poverty that I always thought I would never experience in my entire life.

That decision made me as hopeless as a cancer patient, with nothing around to replenish me, to revive my empty soul and beaten heart except on searching for an escape from everything.

Days passed and we were both trying to fix the typical problems which became hard for me to handle, paralleled with a weird feeling inside.

"Where are you?" Robina asked.
"In the boxing ring, maximum ten minutes and I will start my fight", I answered in a hurry.
"Why you didn't tell me? Why you're hiding such acts on me?"
She nervously questioned.
"Honey, leave me to do things the way I want," was my mean answer.
"But you haven't yet completely recovered, and I didn't see you training again, you're not prepared honey. How come you enrolled in a championship like that? You will harm yourself. Please don't fight." She exclaimed. "I know well what I'm doing, as you also know well that I never prepare for anything. I knew about the championship two days back and asked the coach to register my name. They are calling my name; I will call you later, Robina," was my answer before I entered the ring.

Punching someone legally would console me rather than retaliating against myself for the creature I had become.

The fight started and I began to attack. I gave my opponent no chance to relax; I fought with anger and sadness as a revenge to my destroyed inner self.

My opponent was losing control to my aggressive hits.

All of the audience shouted my name loudly.

I picked up all my powers to finish the first round with confidence. I could hear the audience screaming my name as a sure winner of the second round.

The bell rang; round one was over.

My coach refreshed me with water. He was looking and smiling proudly to his unprepared champ who never betrayed victory.

I felt confident and looked at my friends.

My trainer slapped my shoulder to stand up again before the second round began.

I stood up quickly with a passion to win, but suddenly fell back again on the chair. All I saw was black, and my heart was racing.

The coach held my shoulder and said;

"Are you okay champ? Is there anything wrong?"

I tried to rub my eyes again, and stood up slowly.

"What's there champ? Are you okay?" He repeated.

I looked around well, the image was again clear enough.

"It's okay coach, I'm just benefiting from the break."

I said my words slowly while trying to balance myself.

The coach looked confused, but didn't say anything for his champ who never lost.

The bell rang, "Go champ", he shouted.

The opponent was afraid and kept away waiting for me to attack.

I focused, took slow steps and deeply breathed to finish the round triumphantly.

"Go champ, go champ!" I heard the audience chanting with every hit I did. The audience voices got louder, in contrast to my hits that got softer. My heart throbbed fast as I missed the targets.

The opponent sensed my weakness and took advantage of it to launch a counter attack.

The three-minute round seemed like three months.

I was losing control, and became almost defenceless at his strong punches.

The referee moved me away every time I took advantage to rest while grabbing my opponent tightly. He had showed no mercy to my confused state.

One minute was left for this round.

Victory was going away by my sudden meaningless defence.

I recognized well that something wrong was happening inside, which made me lose my focus.

"I don't want victory, but I don't want to be beaten before all of the spectators," I heard from my inner self calling.

"Excuse me Lord, but I will attack with no rules," was what I said for my Lord.

That minute was enough for me to beat that opponent with no mercy.

I felt the referee touching me again, but this time to separate my opponent who was catching me to have some rest from my aggressive hits.

The bell rang and the fight was over. I did not respect rules, and so the referee raised my opponent's hand because I was being disqualified for illegal attitude. I expected this result, but the audience were again shouting my name loudly as a real winner.

Thank God I wasn't the one beaten, and could leave the ring with a high chin.

I left the university championship worried about my health condition after the fight.

I went to a nearby hospital and asked a doctor about my worrying situation.

His answer was logical. He explained that getting in a championship without training could lead to those symptoms especially with my body, because I was still in need of more rest after the accident that I'd had.

The answer was persuasive, but I didn't entirely agree. I was devastated. However, it secretly changed some parts of my behaviour.

Chapter 3

"Darkness Revealed at a Special Date"

My overall situation was getting difficult; I started behaving as if Robina wasn't in my life. I partially lost control of my responses to the problems I faced. The fear inside was rising. It was something which I had never experienced before.

I went to her house the day after the championship, and on my way, I wondered whether or not I should tell her about my situation.

If I admitted my weakness to Robina, I will shake the great foundations of my loving relationship, and if I kept it secret, then I will break my inner beliefs which I promised to stay true to.

(Being Truthful in Good and Bad situations).

I arrived to her home without a final and reasonable decision, and so I kept on struggling silently.

She looked me in the eyes worriedly, as if reading my mind.

My mind told me to keep silent when she asked, but I had to answer to explain my latest acts.

Her tears fell down her cheeks and almost burned them. She wanted clear answers from her (supposedly) future husband.

I couldn't bear to watch her tears. It was agony to see. Besides, I was surprised at the way I lost control, I had to surrender to my heart which was urging me to confess the truth.

"I'm weak, and I don't know what to say. It is like I'm dying repeatedly, Robina. It's the first time I've experienced this feeling and I'm lost. I can't act or share with you my new weak attitude," I said miserably, crying.

My heart led me to confess without thinking what my mind was worried about. I asked her to understand that I was feeling unusually and surprisingly weak.

I said those words as an injured and bleeding warrior who cried as if watching his family behold his death.

It was a moment of my true feelings coming from deep inside asking for any kind of help from my love just to understand my new reality which I wasn't able to accept.

I felt shameful by showing my tears, but deeply, my heart was relaxed since I spoke the truth.

I was confident to the fact that being truthful was the best thing a person can do to stay alive, even in the worst times of my life.

But unfortunately, that confidence left me as soon as I'd finished complaining and listened to the response of Robina.

I expected no answer, but gazed at her eyes again and silently waited for a comment on what she had heard.

"What should I say for a man who would marry me soon but confessed before that life had never subjected him to fear?

You were the one who always taught me how to face myself in all situations, and to focus only on the bright side of myself. Aren't you the one who said, 'As much as we are breathing, everything would be able to be fixed again'? What should I say to the man who is destroying all the principles that we both believed in?

I suggest that you go and sit alone to remember your words then come back as I knew you four years ago." All those moments, she was perplexed. Would she cry that she'd lost me or would she cry on me because I'd lost myself.

"It seems I'm totally lost now. Even if you disagree, I don't want to be in contact with anyone this week."

"I want to think alone about my life, and then I will come back with a clear answer."

I said those words and went back home, surrounded by darkness.

My heart began to beat fast again, but I ignored it and tried to overcome it by convincing myself that it was only an illusion stemming from the depression, sadness, and grief, I'd permitted to enter my life. I should disregard darkness and focus on hope and optimism. I went home and straight to my bedroom just to have some sleep to regain composure.

But inside, there was no room for relaxation.

"Why I confessed." What have I done to my relationship?

What is Robina thinking about me now?

I'm now the perfect coward to the girl who believed in me as her only strong man.

I should have kept silent.

I should have overcome that depression by ignoring it.

It's nothing more than negative ideas trying to break down my strength.

I have nothing to fear, and I will go back to the person I was before.

I shall prove back to myself and for my love that I'm still the person she knew before.

All those questions and ideas raced in my mind as I lay in bed. As I continued to wonder, my mum interrupted to tell me that my brother and my friends were out on the balcony waiting for me to join them.

I decided in that moment to start open a new page full of hope and optimism. I went outside and sat with them as if nothing had happened.

Every one of them asked about my studies and about the graduation project that used to take most of my time.

The friendly atmosphere was warm, I had really missed sitting with all of them.

But that warmth couldn't continue when some of my close friends asked me about Robina and the details of our wedding.

They were all in a hurry to know the answer.

I tried to answer but one of my friends interrupted,

"Poor Robert, he will miss your wedding. He used to love you so much, and had never stopped talking about the old memories that you both had together.

He loved you more than a brother. We are all sure that he can hear us, and is feeling happy for you."

Those words shocked me.

Robert was my childhood best friend.

May 5th marks the day of his death by a car accident. We were supposed to commemorate him by praying and putting flowers on his grave.

"Look, I still have many pictures of him on my phone, and this a special one of both of you together," my friend said again.

I stood up and asked him to show me the photo, then I stood on the ledge of the balcony to check it alone.

I stared carefully at the picture and checked his face that I missed, then remembered his words, laughs, advice and the worst times we had together.

That picture embodied my lovely past. It made my heart sink wishing him alive.

I recalled those memories alone with that picture. I felt the meaning of loneliness even when I was surrounded by adoring people.

But suddenly, the picture appeared partially black. I thought I was imagining. I tried to concentrate more on it, but in vain. My heartbeats increased dramatically and the picture became totally black.

I realised that I was losing my consciousness, and about to fall off the balcony. I turned quickly to check on my brother and friends, but I lost control and fell to the ground.

Thank God that turning back saved me from falling down to the street. Instead, I fell on the balcony's floor and banged my head against the edge of the ground.

As I gained consciousness, I heard someone saying, "He is okay for now, but he bled so much and fell for no reason. We must keep him for a minimum of three days under close medical surveillance to know what caused the accident." That someone was a doctor talking to my brother in the Emergency room of a nearby hospital.

Realizing that I was officially ill, I worried about my weakness and about the people who would know about that too.

At that time, I asked my brother to inform my family that I was working on my graduation project.

Chapter 4

"My New Painful Secret"

I stayed in the hospital for three days; it was the perfect place to sit alone. My brother and friends came over every day, and I called my mother twice every six hours. Most importantly, I had enough time on my own in order to make my hardest decision which came on the third day after I spoke with the doctor about my medical condition.

"Your case happens to one in every thousand people. The heart doesn't function well. Instead it gives unusual disorders which leads to fast beats every time you are subjected to hard situations.

This case is not genetic, it comes from no specific reason, but it could kill you for many reasons.

You will live normally as any other person, but you must not be subjected to difficult situations or anything that brings about stress. Even donating blood isn't allowed. The heart will react badly in the form of slow or fast beats which could cause shortness of breath and could lead to sudden death.

Your nerves must be always relaxed. Try to be peaceful in everything and take up soft sports to keep exhaustion and fatigue away.

You must adapt yourself to your new situation and to avoid negative ideas and feelings.

You must surround yourself with things that makes you happy. Your heart can be treated if you keep up hope, especially that your case is a chronic syndrome which we still don't have a perfect cure for."

The doctor said his words and looked to hear any question from my side.

"May we keep that sickness as a secret between both of us?

May you never tell my brother or anyone about my case?

If you can, it would be a good impulse to heal myself with your help doctor."

I asked him gently.

"But what should I do with the reports? How can I lie to your guardians about your condition?" He asked in the same way.

"I understand that you should be responsible about being truthful with your patient's parents, but I will appreciate it more if you consider me as a mature person who is wise enough to take care of himself. You will break the heart of my parents and you will kill me twice. Just let it be a secret for my parents' sake. With my strength and motivation I'll get over my disease."

The doctor evaluated my case and gave me his promise. Thus, he explained to my brother that it was only a nervous disorder as a result of high pressure of work and studies simultaneously.

There were two days left to submit my graduation project. I left the hospital and went back home, but surely heard many complaints from my mother who missed me.

I stayed in my bedroom for a day preparing for my graduation project that I had pretended to be doing for the last couple of days.

Well prepared, I stood in the second day before my professors to discuss my project. It wasn't easy at all for I was emotionally and physically destroyed. However, the discussion went smoothly and the doctors were impressed about the presentation. So, they gave me a high grade. I put on a fake smile to keep my spirit high as I recalled the sweet memories I had there before leaving the University for good.

That fake smile was easy to put on for that farewell, yet it was very hard to do while breaking up with my sweetheart.

Chapter 5

"The Ominous Day"

After five days of being alone. I was ready to tell Robina my final decision.

"If you want to leave me, please don't come," was what she answered after I called her on the way.

She was afraid and tried to reconstruct what I was going to destroy.

I was not able to look at her eyes. A feeling of shame filled my inner-self.

She told me that I couldn't come back with a quick decision.

She asked me to tell her later if I wasn't still feeling good.

She tried her best to delay the horrible news she was sure of.

"In bad and good times, we must be truthful." I said then continued,

"That weak person whom you saw five days was still stronger than the one facing you now.

And the one facing you now will be much stronger than the one who would face you in the day after and through your whole life.

My feelings that you thought came from the dark side of myself became strong enough to control me.

Lately, I had started to feel weak in everything I did. I lost all my abilities to face Robina. I hated myself, and really, I wasn't able to handle this relationship anymore.

"It's not my intention to be like this, but this is the truth now.

I'm not ready to be a future husband anymore.

I'm totally destroyed and I really don't want you to be destroyed with me.

You will struggle for a year, two or a little more, but that's better than struggling your whole life with a destroyed person like me.

Save your life from a lost person who stopped being the same man that you knew four years ago.

Call me a betrayer, a coward. Call me whatever you want. Anything would be better than what I'm calling myself. Myself that became my worst enemy. I'm not being able to handle myself anymore, just save yourself Robina."

And please don't say "No", because I'm not able to say yes for you, dear. For God's sake I'm asking you to end this relationship on the right way as we started it."

Searching for words to describe her response was something I couldn't find to write in this book.

"Till death do us part, I will keep loving you", became meaningless like all the other words we had said.

Chapter 6

"Sound & Inspired Decision"

Back to the beginning, my love story was turning into a painful memory that I needed to forget by making a decision for my future. I had decided to travel abroad as I was unable to be within my surroundings at that present time, especially with these people around me.

That decision was inspired from the image of the letter M in the arrangement of the flying pigeons, and indeed the white one mesmerized my heart as if it had talked to me like a sign from God.

"I saw you standing on the balcony for a long time, as if you were speaking with angels.

Tell me son, is it true?" were the words that I heard from my lovely worried mother asking while she entered my gloomy bedroom and sat beside me.

"You will not believe, mother," I answered.

"I watched my initial letter showing in the arrangement of the flying pigeons as if God saluted me with a sweet and a white pigeon which appeared clearly in the flock. It was a good omen."

"Well that's nice, I never noticed it before," she replied. "But you stood so long. Were you thinking of something else son?

I answered with a low voice.

"That image was enough for me to stand so long. It's the only bright image that I still see in my dark present."

"Well, calm down son, you're still too young for that sadness. I can feel that you were struggling alone in the last months without asking us for help. Being an introvert makes us both suffer. So please tell me what's happening and everything will be solved."

She asked worriedly.

But I continued,

"It's too complicated to tell you, but in brief, I can assure that your son has proved to be very foolish.

And surely, the exaggeration about my self-confidence was the key to show my frail reality in facing my dark side."

"What are you saying son?" "What do you know about darkness?"

"It's a sort of illusion. You're definitely overstating the word darkness," my mother interrupted. "I'm not, mother", I answered. "Darkness is enveloping my life lately. Everything is going badly with me."

"My feelings, my attitude, my thoughts and hopes are all changing. I almost numb. I barely feel anything.

But she interrupted again.

"Calm down son and tell me. Maybe, I can solve your problems, everything has a solution. Just try to believe again in yourself. With God's blessing we will both find the solutions."

I smiled at her innocence, then uttered,

"I want to travel mother. Travel to a faraway place. To the place where I can solve and handle everything alone."

"Please don't speak like that. We are all by your side, and everything is going to be okay," she repeated.

"It will be much better if I am alone. I'm tired enough mother."

"What do you mean by traveling and alone? Do you want to leave us son? And what about Robina? How would you solve that decision with her?" She questioned me.

"It's okay for Robina; the relationship will not disturb my idea of traveling. We broke up today mother, and by the time I was on the balcony, the idea of traveling occurred to me."
"I do not believe what you are saying.

Please look at me. Problems make us blind, and distort our thoughts and the ability to face our problems.

Speaking out your secrets to someone close will comfort you. You become so miserable alone. Just tell me and we will fix everything together," she cried out.

"It's over now, everything is finished. I made my decision, and I'm convinced in what I did. It's a little late to mend what I damaged."

"What happened?" She asked loudly. "Please tell me son, she is also like my daughter, and I'm sure that she is now broken like you." She hugged me as if begging me to tell her that I was lying.

"Mother", I answered, "She is still the same. She did nothing wrong, but I'm the one who changed and started to see her wrong in every simple action. I am not able to love or even to cure myself.

I'm totally wasted, as if I'm in the middle of nowhere. It's not fair for her to suffer with me, and if we continue, she will be wrecked too."

"Just stop that," she intervened nervously. "You are speaking as if you are going to die; stop speaking in that way son. You're not the first one who failed in handling his problems.

You can cure yourself and make the relationship work again, I know you can; you're too strong for those bloodcurdling words."

"I know full well what I'm doing", I said again. "I thought extensively before I ended things, just don't worry about her because time will be enough to heal everything. She will be in pain for a year or two, maximum three, but that's much better than being hurt all her life."

"Stop that silly talking! That girl is not a game, and that's not you speaking. Just tell me, what's really happening?" She asked again angrily.

"I've changed mother, I'm not the person I used to be. The man you saw previously in your son has failed in facing life. I'm not able to face myself anymore.

It was a wrong decision to have a serious relationship at an early age. And time has proved that for me.

I loathe my old decisions as I hate myself every moment I think about that decision.

Please understand me mother," I repeated.

"What should I understand son?

I can't believe that I'm looking into the same eyes which showed the confidence of a responsible man, who brought along a new girl to our family, and here you are now speaking as a child who wants a new life traveling.

But, I only have one thing to say, it seems you were a child when you decided to get engaged to her.

This is not you talking. Think again carefully my son; God is watching everything. This is not the way a truthful person behaves. Your words, and your promises are the main factors that build your character and everything else is secondary. That girl is your fiancé and you both love each other". She said.

"Because of that, I have the right to say 'No' and in the name of God", I interrupted.

"You don't know anything about God. He doesn't tell you to surrender in that selfish way. People's hearts cannot to be manipulated like that.

A man must be strong to fight for his words instead of running away from his responsibility.

I feel down. The man I used to see inside you evaporated. I am crying for the girl who loved the man who preferred to escape on the expense of her broken heart.

I love you both son, but I don't know how I should mend what you don't want to cure anymore.

That's your choice; do whatever you want, but know well son, that God will give no mercy for your actions, later if you saw anyone of us dying, be sure that you were the reason because when a person stabs someone's heart, God will do the same and more with the ones he loves."

"You don't know anything mother" I stopped her again to confess the main reason.

"You said everything son.

I'm really confused about you. I know you are strong enough to stand tall, but I'm worried about the girl whom we all loved. Just pray my son, pray for God to forgive you on the pain you caused to her."

Those words were enough for me to leave home. I couldn't look in anyone's eyes. I felt ashamed of being unable to say the truth.

I was not able to walk long distances. Darkness was getting closer. My only direction was towards my neighbour, Mrs. Elizabeth)

She was an old Lady who has understood me since childhood. She differed from my mother being a person who solved her problems by using her logic and heart together.

She was wise enough to read my buried feelings. She was a supportive mother.

I sat silently, without knowing how to start. I didn't want to tell anyone about my health problem, but I was fed up enough of everything that I was about to explode from the massive pain I'd never experienced before.

I continued like that for couple of minutes, as a guilty child who had no words to justify the tears which started to appear in my red eyes.

"Your eyes remind me of myself son."

She broke the silence, while sitting aside and looking outside the window as if she had travelled in time to a similar situation that she solved in her own way.

"I used to have that look 20 years ago. It was simply my hardest time with nothing except the miracles I clung to.

In that time, everyone saw me disconnected from people. I was in my own cocoon.

My situation was so hard to explain, but it was titled by the words of the doctors who said that my elder son will soon die from a car accident that put him in a coma", Elizabeth recalled.

I became confused. My mind was unable to control the responses of my broken heart which objected the idea of losing someone it loved.

She continued, "All started to prepare me for the funeral of my clinically dead son. That idea was fair enough to kill me twice at every moment I lived.

I felt weak and everything became meaningless for me.

Killing myself was much easier than watching my child waiting for death.

Praying and counting on hope was what kept me alive in those crucial events.

I believed more in miracles, and searched for every word that spoke about God. I listened to his words and had surrendered my heart and son to him.

I never stopped praying, and never regretted anything for everything happens at his ultimate will. All said that I became crazy for that strong belief in those small words before the big ones.

I changed my life to thank God for all his blessings and on every grace he gave us in times I was blind to the enlightenments he granted me.

As also, I thanked him for my craziness and confessed that I'm convinced of any judgment which will only come through his will.

I felt twisted until someone came and explained that being crazy is only allowed in the Love of the Lord.

And showed that my imaginary world that I craved for was the real one.

He was a good person who came to the hospital after he knew about the car accident which happened near his house.

That person was known as a doctor, but different from all others. He entered the child's room with an intention to show me that I was not alone exaggerating in loving the Lord.

He truly lightened me on the fact that everything is done by the will of God.

He clarified that every trouble we go through, is a blessing to awaken us on the strength of goodness inside.

He convinced me that exaggerating about the power of God is the best thing a person can do.

He asked me to continue living in that world- world of prayers and tranquillity-and gave me his bracelet.

His words were my motivation and my strength in the darkest time. I loved those words and continued to believe that the one who gives us every breath is not disturbed by our daily problems that seem the end of the world to us.

I lived in the world of hope which truly gave me the power of patience. This enabled me to see my son opening his eyes again after around three months of unconsciousness as a miracle which doctors couldn't understand." "Was that from the bracelet?" I interrupted. "Well, it depends on what I believed son", was her answer.

"Your memories nourished my soul, but those eyes that you noticed in me are asking whether I should travel or not.
I came here to ask for advice. I feel down, shamed about my weak initiative in facing problems and I really want to know if traveling is something considered as escaping from reality. Can you interpret it in another way?"
I asked with better eyes.
"So you want to leave me alone son?" She asked gently. "I just want to relax, my dear." I answered.
"Have you thought through that decision?" She repeated.
"Yes, and I can say that it's the only decision left keeping me standing." I replied.
"Well, let me tell you something son, and think well about it", she replied with her eyes focused on mine.

"We all know about the eagles and how they are powerful. We all think that they are born powerful, and stay this way throughout life until they die, right?" "Yes, I think that's true." I replied.

"Wrong," she said with a tough look and kept silent for a moment to catch all my attention towards what she was going to say.

"Every forty years, an eagle becomes old and so weak, it cannot fight as it used to.

It becomes unable to handle its kingdom and for that reason, it flies to a far place. A far place to hide within a community with no eagles, only rocks and small animals around to feed on.

This eagle will take off its feathers using its beak which will later break by hitting it on a rock, then it will wait for many months to produce new feathers and to renew its beak. This will grow much stronger than before and will go back to its kingdom to fly again as the kings of the sky. We always think they're strong while they pass through ups and downs.

Weakness hits all creatures, few are those who know how to deal with until they restore power.

Your daring step to leave your country to cure yourself is very honourable. It's better than living here weakly.

It doesn't depend on the place as much as it does on how truthful you are son.

I wish all others could understand that wisdom as you can.

I'm sure that this bracelet will remind you of that eagle inside you.

Just keep it with you as a gift from your second mother." she said while putting it gently in my hand.

"I'm so thankful for you, mum, but I can see the letters M & H printed on it. Are they related to someone? Or they belong to a special principle to be obeyed?" I asked with a look of curiosity after wearing that lovely bracelet.

"Those letters surely have a meaning, and the one who gave it to me knows more how to explain. I will lead you to his place in a near village, and I'm sure that he would help better than your aged mother," was her lovely answer.

Chapter 7

"Spiritual Knowledge"

Losing self-control was the main reason to search for help from the ultimate Power. Consequently, I indulged myself to learn more about God's words.

I read many books about God, and attended all the places in which He was praised.

Following the Creator's words with love to put me on the right track to have my soul purified and purged to meet the Lord by a purified soul.

When we speak about the Creator, we talk about how loyal we are and sure that he is always with us.

We must have Love as the only way to face even our enemies, then to accept all pains which is definitely a result of our bad behaviours.

Because we reap what we sow. Instead we should smile for the pain and love our enemies. If we hate our enemies, we become enemies of ourselves, then we gain no favour.

Abiding by the words of God was done under the following motto:

"If You Believe then You Obey."

Following these beliefs must be done without thinking about others' intentions and thoughts of our weaknesses. Instead, we must be working to strengthen the bond with the Lord who tests our priorities either by choosing to be blind, or in being like saints who believed that goodness is always stronger than evil and that darkness will disappear at the time we light a candle inside.

The candle inside is the sound of God living in everyone, it's only touched by going back to a child's innocence , and child's innocence means that your heart can only know love.

Traveling was the best means to help me purify my soul and keep me away from my mother country, and away from the recurrent struggles with new people who know nothing about my painful background.

But before, knowing the secret of that bracelet taken from Elizabeth- made me curious to meet that wise person who became my spiritual supporter.

Chapter 8

"The Support"

I went to a near village to meet that person. I was so keen to know more about the Lord from his experience.

I knocked the door and waited holding the papers of my medical results preparing myself for the hopeful man inside.

The door was opened by a lovely elderly person who asked me to come in.

His face was so peaceful but I couldn't see his eyes as they were covered by dark glasses.

"Enter son, please take a seat. Just give me two minutes, I'm preparing my green tea, do you want some?" he asked gently.

"No thanks, I will wait for you, take your time Doctor."

Then, I stepped inside and assessed the apartment.

It was bright and colourful, and perfectly organized.

The seats, the books, curtains and even the smell was as if in nature.

"So, you are that guy who stole my bracelet?" He asked with a welcome smile.

"Yes, I'm that thief who is bringing back what had been stolen." I answered.

"You were smart to steal something so expensive, but if I were you, I would never had thought of giving something so valuable back to its owner." he answered peacefully.

"If this will make me back who I am, then I would pay you my life as a bonus." I answered sadly.

"Oh come on son, just tell me what's in your heart. And what are those papers that you're holding?"

I leaned close silently and gave him the papers, then sat back and started to speak,
"My life is changing badly, doctor.
I'm not the person I used to be. Weakness became my only feeling. I'm totally lost and cannot handle my life anymore.
Screams of death are heard loud inside, and no one is understanding my struggle. I'm feeling lonely, just trying to redeem my life by following the Lord's words.
I'm living depressed and aimless days with nothing to make me happy. I'm really tired Doctor, feeling down as if the whole world is collapsing on me.
I've missed my strength, I've missed my joy.
I missed the life I used to have.

My mind stopped on functioning except in times I try to apply the words of God and as if trying to be a saint. I became living an imaginary world with the thirst of knowing about light but in a way of preparing myself to face the Lord.

That feeling is increasing, and I just want to know more about being on the right way, maybe because I'm sensing my end.
I came here for guidance. God's path became my sole hope to survive."

"Calm down son", he interrupted gently my monologue. "It seems you're exaggerating. It's not the end of the world. Maybe you're still young, but it's fair enough for a mature man like you to know that your troubles are merely a test."

"A test?" I asked.
"Yes dear," he answered with a pure confident smile.

"Our life is a test, every situation we face is a test. Being weak is a test, same as being strong.
Everything we are subjected to is a test depending on everyone's sins and ability to handle, but the most important is to be aware of that son.
It seems clearly you experienced the feeling of power which was surely your priority. Well, having power as a priority builds a wall between a man and his peaceful inner which distance him from the Creator especially when he chooses his own benefits on the words of God.

Well, surely you were tested in those times. I don't know how much you made fun of others and hurt them. How much you were aggressive with your surround, and how much you betrayed or broke promises by selfish decisions to have satisfaction.
I don't even know how much you enjoyed your powers, forgetting the one who gave it to you".

I didn't utter a word, and continued listening.
"Humans are blessed with a power that could change the world. But when we start thinking about power as our own, we become overwhelmed with confidence. And we secretly detach ourselves from the Creator.
Being courageous with others is something wonderful, but it's the most dangerous when it goes on God's words.
I'm certain that your previous self rarely remembered God's words. That's why it's normal for a person like you

to have feelings of loss and weakness." He was speaking as if reading my past with nothing to answer except,

"If this is true, then what should I do.?"
He answered while staring straight from his dark glasses:

"Orient your inner powers to the right way son".

"How?" I repeated.
"First you must believe that all what you own from powers goes to the Lord. Your ego must be destroyed by giving your own a title of serving the Goodness inside, and serving Goodness must be done as if you're watching the Lord in front, and living like that will give you the intention to be truthful in everything you do. It's all done from that perspective, just living the world on your truth. Whatever you're doing, you must do it truthfully. You will have chances to hesitate and to refuse responsibility as most of people do.

But instead you will be giving your best in being the best son, best student, best employee, best friend, best brother and later on the best husband and father.

Being truthful isn't by saying true words only, but on being true with the words of God.

It will be difficult to do later on, but it will go easy when you give it all of your focus.

Our intentions of living are what evaluates us, and a real man always differentiates perfectly between his priorities.

Being truthful goes above everything else, son.

Rare are the ones who get aware with those things. Those kinds of people give no care for the hardness of tests they face, and that's because they are totally convinced that everything happens by the Will of God.

Those people are the best for God and choosing to be one of them depends on your will.

You will discover more about yourself while being subjected to hard times, where your intentions will be tested if it would stay on believing that the words of God are always above everything."

"It's always like that" I interrupted.

"I appreciate your enthusiasm to the Lord's words but I would appreciate more if you don't give up to the powers inside you." He commented and continued, "Humans are of high inner powers, but most live lost because they ignore it. Instead they search outside themselves leading them into thinking that it is the end of the world.

The same for nuclear power, if you treat a uranium rock as an ordinary one and throw it on a glass, it would have only the power to break it, but if you give consideration to its inner truth of the uranium rock and go inside to stimulate it, then it would have the power to destroy a whole country.

I think you're understanding me, son." He said appreciating my listening.

"Going to the inner, depends on believing in the goodness inside which is a path discovered similar to any other path and more."

He stopped for a moment and drank a little from his green tea cup then continued.

"When you want to be a Martial Art Champion, you try to think and act as Bruce Lee did.

And when you try to be a philosopher, you seek the words of Plato and Aristotle."

"The same for music, you try to feel how Beethoven and Bach used to feel while playing their symphonies."

"You will ask for Bill Gates' ideas in times you seek for money as you ask for the feeling and the thoughts of Alexander in times you seek the path of Greatness.

'I judge myself before being judged', well it's a proverb that I can't forget said by the Great Alexander as an obeying worshipper to the Lord.

He was really one of the best role models of the ancient history.

You're not one of those idols, but you are a human being, and humans always look up for an idol to compare themselves to through times they seek any similar path.

And so, that's the idea I'm trying to clarify, son. Being truthful is a path which will let you pass by its heroes.

Its heroes are the Prophets and Saints who accepted pain and touched their inner peace through the hard times to show us that light could make miracles in times of darkness.

I'm pretty sure that you're not a Saint," he gave a wink from under his dark glasses, then continued

"But I'm sure that a day will arrive and you will overcome what you're still not adapted to."

"The Lord seekers are the same, but they only differ in one thing.

They accept the Lord's will and work as much as they can on applying his words."

"Is that what the letters M & H means on your bracelet?" I asked.

He stared down at the bracelet and was silent for a second, not only in respect of my smart interruption, but as if thinking of the times he used to wear it.

"When you ask for the Lord, the Lord must be everything for you. In every desire, in every act and thought, you must be feeling him and trying to move and solve your problems according to his words as if watching him in front of you.

Being a Lord seeker requires you to have the Lord as the only Master of your heart.

And as we know, we are connected to the Lord only by our hearts. But a heart could love the devil the same or more than loving the one who created it through attractive sins that seems to be a better choice than the right path.

Your heart must love the Lord through loving the world, and complete your family with the right partner on the right way under the name of God.

By so, the mind will keep you safe from sins every time you look at the letters M & H on the bracelet to remember that my heart's priority is always asking for the love of the Lord."

"Well, that's nice to hear". I interrupted.

"Look son, God is a source of love and happiness, he doesn't love to see us weak, but unfortunately, most of the times, God subjects us to troubles letting us feel weak and lonely in order to be nearer of him, because those are the main keys that destroy the ego as also to remember and to depend on him in everything.

Poor humans! They only remember God in times of need and weakness.

Well, that bracelet belonged to me, and I offered it for a dear person who was seeking the Lord. And she knew well that this bracelet should be only in the hands of those who respect God's words.

Well, I respect what she saw in you, and I agree with her about the kind-hearted person inside you.

Maybe you will go outside and blame yourself for listening to an old man, but later, you will remember my words, and I'm sure you will try to apply them, because you are really a truthful person, and those words are showing nothing more than your own truth, son."

I didn't comment, in a way I was urging him to continue his talk because my desire was to be cured, not more.

"It's enough for today, take my number and call me when you want.

If you continue on living in darkness outside, then it means you didn't remember anything except the darkness of my glasses.

But if you start noticing bright things around, then it means you are remembering and feeling the Lord that we spoke about."

He commented on my silence as if focusing on the quality of his words more than the quantity.

But somehow, the second part was meaningless to me, since I couldn't notice anything bright around.

Really, his glasses were not easy to forget.

"I don't offer medicine, I just speak the words that I feel could help to cure your pain.

But whatever happens, remember well that God's words are always above everything.

Don't forget that son," he was saying his words and looking at me straight, lowering his head as if showing what he was hiding. His strong sharp eyes appeared and shocked me in reading my whole inner with a lovely smile.

"It was nice to meet you doctor", I said perplexed.

"Please, don't call me doctor, you're like my son, just call me Sam, I'm like your father; that's if you don't mind."

"I respect your kindness", I answered with a smile

"I will steal your medical papers with no aim to give it back, because they will be meaningless after being compared to the coming ones.

The bracelet is now yours, keep on wearing it son, it will be a reminder of our conversation."

Hope was what I felt while finishing the meeting with that old wise man. Mrs. Elizabeth was pretty smart to arrange a meeting with a person who proved what I thought about being a supportive man.

I went back home, thinking about his words that were similar and stronger from what I believed.

I kept walking and thought more about my decision as a way to search for light through my only hope, in a trip to the dark unknown.

Chapter 9

"Traveling into the Dark Unknown"

And that's what happened later after I rejected many offers. It was a wonderful coincidence that occurred at the moment; I signed an offer to a school atAbu Dhabi (UAE), and then wanted to scan the contracts at a computer centre. But while loading the scanned copies, I received a call directly from a Principal of a school in Dubai I applied to previously. I was surprised to have the call in those moments especially after I waited for them for two weeks.

I listened to her words, prepared myself to reject her offer before sending my contracts to the school in Abu Dhabi.

But, I was shocked when she said that my passport copy which I sent her school before made her recognize that my parents lived with her in the same compound in Kuwait a long time ago; for more than thirteen years.

This means that she knew my parents before I was born twenty three years ago.

The principal and her husband were so interested in my CV and praised my parents for raising a smart guy like me, and insisted that I accept their job offer and to reject others.

I immediately called my parents and told them everything. They were glad to hear about the lovely coincidence.

"She was the sweetest friend ever", was their comment on the principal.

I came back home after I sent the new scanned contracts to Dubai. The contract was of a smaller salary than the one of Abu Dhabi. But surely I called and apologized to the other school and explained that having a principal as a friend of the family in a foreign country is a better choice for me than having a good salary in any other place. I was convinced that receiving support abroad, was my priority, because living with peace of mind was all what I was seeking for.

My Graduation party was missed. I took my certificate, picked up my stuff, and travelled to meet my new someone who could be my family in a foreign country without them knowing anything about my character and what I was going through.

I flew to Dubai to forget my misery, and to cure myself secretly.

My decision wasn't that easy. I was weak and with no passion to live but work hard to accept the Lord's will within a new surrounding, where no one knew a thing about my stressful background.

Chapter 10

"The New Surrounding"

First, I met the principal who showed kindness and respect for the old friendship she had with my parents.

She asked me about all my family members.

She was a good person. She warmly welcomed me and told me to feel at home, well, school.

I showed her an old picture that my mother gave me that she had kept for so long.

The picture showed my parents and the principal with her husband riding horses.

She was astonished when she saw it, and recalled the memories she had with my parents.

She yearned for the past days, and commented about the time they all rode horses and said that she was braver than her husband and dared to ride the horse first. She then showed him how brave she was once again, and travelled to Dubai to open a school with the help of some close relatives.

I wondered how she shared those memories with me and even how she commented on her daring decisions to run her own business without giving consideration to her husband's opinion. Instead, I continued to believe the kindness of the sweetest friend my parents ever told me about.

I had sat with most of the teachers within a week and tried to work with them as one team.

They were so many and counted around two hundred. It was a very big school.

I thought that maybe the huge number of teachers would be an obstacle for the good teamwork I used to have previously, especially when I noticed many of them avoiding contact with me as someone new.

I didn't care for them as much as I loved my work.

I totally believed that the way to success in my spiritual duties depends on how truthful I was with God. It became clear that this way needed a better community for a higher self-evaluation.

It turned out that the quality of teachers, not their number hindered teamwork at the school. Most of them were working only for economical needs and were only teaching to get their salaries at the end of the months. They didn't care for the loyalty of work.

They always blamed other good teachers for their own faults and lack of responsibilities, and never taught well in class so that their students would need to pay them for private tutoring. "Tutoring is forbidden to be done outside the school," was what the Principal said in the first teacher's meeting of the year.

This concept wasn't taken into consideration. Most of the teachers smiled sarcastically at the principal mocking her naive rules.

I didn't intend to know, but later, I discovered that most of the teachers tutored outside the school and surprisingly via the principle, as if she was illegally giving financial benefits for teachers who weren't loyal to her.

I didn't believe in my horrible image of that principal. She was so kind in the first meeting and always replied with lovely words whenever I met her.

I kept on working truthfully and stopped caring about what I saw in my new surroundings.

I insisted on showing love as my only way to face all my conflicts, even to my enemies. Having that experience made me see people of different sorts and backgrounds.

I noticed how most of the teachers, lied to one another and back-stabbed their closest friends because earning money required that they become experts in lying and indifferent to the Creator's Limitations.

They were perfect slaves for their meaningless aims.

They covered their lies by wicked smiles to hide their phony characters. Some of them used to show artificial warmth for any stranger to get his trust then would run their mouths to disclose that teacher's secrets and privacy.

They evaluated themselves based on a materialistic level and their closeness with the owners of the school and the administration.

Those people were wicked in their acts and never were true to themselves. They worked to develop themselves as books of business and fashion, and only felt satisfied when fake society showered them with false compliments and praise.

The word 'Truthful' was clearly a joke to them.

God was something to remember only while praying, not in their practical days.

They forgot that all saints left life's luxury, which they were able to have easily, to live humbly and truthfully and to praise the Lord. That was their only aim.

They made God abstract, never concrete in their actions. He was remembered once a week just for forgiveness, and to forget about all the other days.

Days were passing slowly and I observed new and unexpected happenings.

Even my regards weren't replied to anymore by the principle, who tried to show me that she was the absolute ruler whom I must obey at her school.

I realized that I was mistaken in dealing with others according to the view of my parents who had met her twenty-three years ago.

The sweetest friend ever had changed with time. I recognized finally that the warmth the principal showed to my family was nothing but a business transaction to add me to the number of teachers at her school. Her school made by materialistic and psychopathic egos.

"Who follows me, never walks in darkness." was what I memorized and repeated internally while digesting the words of God.

I understood that the hypocrisy and inauthenticity were the darkness itself and honesty was the light I craved.

Those people and I were walking different tracks.

Fighting with a gun in the battlefield was much easier than being a 'warrior of light' surrounded by artificial blind people.

It was so hard to adapt myself in this society. I realized that the hardship I was living in Dubai was rather better than the tribulations I was going to have in my country.

The community at my school considered me like any other person without any single idea about my painful history.

Within that status quo. I was in dire need for someone supportive, and surely Mr. Sam was the best one to call.

Chapter 11

"The Fateful Call"

I was back home. I went up to the roof of my house and called Mr. Sam to have his advice again about my health update.

"Hi Sam. I just remembered you and wanted to salute you as a new person with a new life."

"Well, it felt so long waiting to hear your voice son. Just tell me about you."

He answered warmly.

"I'll always remember you and your words that have helped me so much. But my plans are not very successful, because the surrounding isn't that good.

Most of them are materialistic, and have no appreciation to any of the words that we talked about.

They are the opposite. They are so ridiculous. They are cowards; they care less for their weakness, they care only for money.

I hate no one, and no one hates me as long as I'm not from the administration staff and not challenging them to take their students and tutor them.

Imagine the type of people, they only fear losing money. I didn't tell them about the previous friendship between my parents and the principal to avoid being one-sided. I didn't want to count on anyone but myself.

I can visualize what you told me about egoism embodied in the principal who became very arrogant and boastful after running her own school.

I told my family nothing about them except that they replied the salutation.

I'm not happy in my life here, but the best for me is that no one knows anything about my past. That is giving me inner security to relax from such a responsibility.

The school is so big and the only event that I feared most was a woman I met who is married from a man in my village.

I never saw her before, but she knows all my previous community, and I'm afraid of being in contact with her.

I'm doing my best to stay away from her, especially after I noticed that she is betraying her husband with a young teacher who is already engaged and going to marry in the coming summer.

I feel disgusted from their act. I can't see a betrayer before my eyes, Sam.

There are many other cheaters that I noticed by daily coincidences."

Feeling isolated in my new situation led me to explain everything clearly, and I was eager to hear Mr. Sam's advice.

"Well, I loved your description for what you're newly facing, but as we said previously, God gives us the feeling of weakness in order to open a door of dependence on his power and greatness in everything." Mr Sam said.

"Trying to adjust oneself in that situation is something wonderful which only strong men can achieve, but through that adjustment, you will be tested about how much God's words mean to you. Be sure those couples are a part of the test which you are passing through.

Be careful son, because sometimes we do the same things we hate most in others.

But here it goes to the level of being aware about God's words either to obey them continuously or to follow secretly the choice of the couples which disgust you for now."

"I don't understand how God can subject a fiancé and another husband to be betrayed by their partners just to show me an example! "I replied angrily.

"Son, surely you're not the reason. You're just watching those couples harvest what they planted previously as bad decisions they made about their lives.

Maybe they were both materialistic and married or engaged for that sake.

And maybe they were truthful, but being subjected to tempting choices while facing problems, changed their desires and made them betrayers.

We don't know perfectly the reasons as it's not our duty to know, but being exposed to such events would be a big test for you not to be sick of yourself if you thought or did something similar as those people did."

"What do you mean by that, Mr. Sam?

I'm not that kind of person. Infidelity was never and wouldn't ever be in my life." I replied as if being insulted especially because he focused only on that idea.

"Calm down son, I'm not saying that you are an infidel, but I'm just clarifying some of the ways God puts us to trial.

It's when the test targets the heart's desires, where a person will be subjected to love, but with somebody who doesn't rightfully and ethically belong to him. That test will show how much the person's heart will obey the words of God.

Truthful people like you aren't materialistic, so your trials will be mostly emotional.

Therefore, here goes the best trials of God, which is perfectly targeting feelings and Mind orders.

Definitely, a person cannot succeed unless he looks by the feelings and intentions of a Sister, Mother or Daughter to any close colleague he would have.

But what is astonishing, is surely not the one who fails as those couples who truly followed the hunger of their hearts, but to the ones who follow their mind orders by directing the heart's hungers and desires to the name of God's words," he said the last words slowly.

"Doctor, you're still focusing on something that I would never do, and I repeat, I'm not that kind of person you're thinking of." I interrupted again.

"Even if you're not from the type of people who do such sins, it's never a mistake to listen to advice from an old man who loves you like I do, son.

I don't want you to feel uneasy again, it was an idea I felt would happen with you and just focused on it.

I answered that phone call because I love to speak with truthful people like you.

Being honest needs a person to stay always aware for everything and to ignore his certainty of being safe from mistakes.

Remember well, that God categorizes people as metals depending on how much they apply his non obligatory words. It's always a person's decision to choose which kind of metal he wants to be.

And I'm sure that being Gold like you needs a continuous awareness of your daily behaviours son."

I couldn't distinguish if the last comment was an apology or insistence on his point of view about what he saw in my character. Anyway, I felt insulted and misunderstood.

His words gave me an impression that Mr. Sam was too traditional for this modern world. He was old and different from the one who had cured my lovely neighbour twenty years ago.

I clearly felt that in this call, he was the one speaking about dark ideas and things that I would never do and which was not even the aim of my call.

It was the toughest call ever which I had after my travel. I felt completely lonely, especially that he was one whom I thought of as helpful and understanding. He became like most of my past surrounding and more, just giving an ideal and philosophical advice instead of helping me to stand in my present dark life.

I asked God to give me patience to accept that path without objections, and to help me treat my loneliness with anyone who could be seeking the same beliefs in Dubai.

Sitting up on the roof was enough for me to be alone with the Creator. It was the place I used to feel peace and tranquillity through those moments.

I continued my days working in that obnoxious school in the hope that God would let me accept his will.

I used to go up to the same roof every night to sit alone and review and sensibly judge myself if I hesitated through my attitude in my daily acts.

And really, that roof became my best friend. I felt that God was hearing every single prayer that I said.

Living in darkness was an obligatory experience to attain a wisdom for my new sick character.

All I needed at that time was a smile from someone to make me feel that I belong to my new reality- my new status quo.

Chapter 12

"Adaptation to the Dark Unknown"

Sharing my time with my students was the best solution. They were so lovely, pure-hearted and innocent. Sometimes, they caused me headache, especially when they asked about their previous teacher whom they seemed to love more than a new strict one like me.

But even though, I kept on trying to approach them and to live their lives by discussing with them their desires and their daily problems.

I loved sitting with them on every break remembering the times I was a youth at their age, running and imagining a bright future full of hope and aiming to be happy while achieving being the one I dreamt about.

Dealing with truthful innocent kids was something I loved much more than sitting with most of the phony teachers.

The recesses became my happy times while roaming out freely in the playground with my students as my kids or small brothers and sisters.

Those small kids were not easy. They opened their hearts for me. Likewise, they wanted me to open my heart for them too.

They went on asking me if I was in a relationship, and if I was going to get married soon.

Well, I preferred to sit alone when they asked me such questions because I had no words to answer those little pupils.

They also used to ask me to play football with them, but I refused to join by an excuse that I didn't know how to play the game I was professional at.

On the contrary, most of the teachers played as beginners, with my students, and boasted about being sportive thinking that I had no sport experience.

Later, I used to sit alone under the sunshine, traveling to another world, as if absorbing the direct charge from the Lord under that hot sun.
Then, as usual, I came back home depressed. My bed became the second best friend for I spent a lot of time lying on it.

I called my parents every day, but my phone kept silent for long time- I received no calls from people who loved me.

I was surrounded by darkness as I was only a body without a soul. I was partially dead.

Chapter 13

"The Showing up of Someone White"

Throughout my struggles and while living in the gloomy unknown, something else was happening.

"Among the eagle's plans, flew a graceful white pigeon."

"Is that you? The one whom all the students told me about. I really wish I was your student too."

Well that was the first compliment, I ever say to a new girl as a colleague teacher who was still in my country for a couple of weeks after I travelled to Dubai. This woman was outside Dubai through the first couple of weeks of the teaching year (For a specific reason), but then, she came back again to teach her classes in the same department where I was already taking one of her classes.

"You are cheating by explaining the lessons quickly", she said when I started my new life as a mathematics teacher for lower grades.

"I swear I didn't know", I answered.

She childishly told the coordinator that I'm a kid who doesn't know how to follow the curriculum.

"Hey son, how are you today? We are going to start in this lesson," she said meanly.

"It's okay, start with the lesson you want", I answered with a smile.

The other day, she approached me,

"Hey son, how are you today? "We must start in this lesson," she also commented,
"My grandmother used to say, 'Laughing without a reason is impolite.'" She uttered that like a small girl who asks others to give her respect in the name of humanity.

"First, I respect what your grandmother used to say, but who told you I'm laughing with no reason." I replied.
"Really, so tell me what's the reason?" She asked.

"Just stop saying 'My Son', please." I answered.

"Is it something to laugh at? My son?" She repeated.

I smiled back, "You can continue saying that as much as you like, but be careful because later I will start asking for my rights as your son. But I think today we shall start in the lesson you spoke about yesterday," was my answer while walking away from her class as she was going to kill me with her angry eyes.

She entered my class the day after and tried to mess around with my students who previously were her students.

But I did the same and came back to her class in the following day and informed her students of having a free period as a decision of revenge taken by my own.

She understood my joke while her class turned messy and noisy.

She tried to start all over with me forgetting the teasing. She surrendered to the fact that I was going to treat her the same way she was treating me.

As far I was concerned. I only cared for a smile from any source to cheer myself.

Joking, smiling and sharing similar moments increased peacefully as the days passed by.

A new stage of peace was entering my life again, and somehow she watered my dry soul every time we argued.

I showed her a "Mwah" beside her name when I saved her number on my phone. Similarly, she did the same when a daily smile on my lesson plan appeared every morning.

My life was turning bright by the smile from a childish innocent colleague as if a candle that came to lit up in the darkness- the abstract unknown.

Later, we were sitting in the teachers' room and some nosy teachers asked about her salary.

She got afraid and maintained silence like a threatened little girl waiting her punishment.

"I know the administration doesn't allow anyone to speak about his salary, as I don't want to know about yours, but dear, don't be afraid of others. One should fear God only." I commented as I smiled at her innocence in exaggerating fear while dealing with other evil people.

"You are the first one I see at school sitting under the sun as I do. Although your complexion isn't that white, taking Vitamin D is so important to your well-being." Was her comment on my usual sitting in the sunny playground.

I liked her lovely idea which never came across my mind and took it as the best reason to explain the underlying reality- spiritual contemplation, then answered.

"Finally, someone was able to understand the reason behind my sitting under the scorching sun."

But she continued her predictions,

"It seems you're obsessed with your health. I can notice that as well as the charm that never leaves your hand."

"Well that's true; I had it from a sweet person to remind me to take care of myself," I answered while putting my hand on the bracelet then I continued,

"I wish a day will come and you will have a similar bracelet but without sitting under the hot sun in a far place."

"I think I understood, but I have class and I must move dear," was her answer with a curious look in her eyes.

On another day, after the recess ended, and while the students were entering their classes, an aged teacher fell to the ground and passed out. It was a result of excessive fatigue and overload at school. I quickly left my students and rushed to help her; I lift her to a safe area.

Then, I went inside to ask the teachers to help in what they had already seen outside. But unfortunately, they didn't care for their colleague and claimed that they were very busy. I darted outdoors after I failed to get help to see what I could do with the sick teacher. However, and to my surprise, she was already walking to the nurse's room with the help of my innocent math teacher.

On another day, during the break, I told her that I'm going to the second building after we were sitting together. I turned then moved away. Later I saw the students running in the opposite direction and saying her name with fear.

I turned back to check what happened and saw her still sitting but shaking and crying from a flying football kicked by a stupid student.

I ran for help, but she wept and darted to the bathroom to hide her tears, without saying a word.

After a while, I searched for her to check how she was.

I checked the nurse's room, then the teacher's room, but couldn't find her. I passed by her class to check who replaced her in class. I was surprised to see her in class again continuing the lesson normally but with a red stamp on her face from the ball shot and as if nothing happened

I laughed at her oversensitivity in such situations. She was amazing and was acting as peaceful as the person I wanted to be. Her acts was translating God's words into reality. She made me notice the pure transparent girl inside her.

That girl was opposite to her size. She was taller than me, and that was obvious for all.

Even my students noticed that difference, and later one of them told me that I'm wearing boots to match her height.

She told me even while we were sitting at the threshold of the teacher's room.

"Poor you"

"How dare you speak with me and forget that God created you short and you still need three to four centimetres in order to talk me as a gentleman"

Surely I was not that short, but she was taller than me by three centimetres. Anyways, I laughed at her funny innocent jokes and went back to my class to teach my lovely students who shared with her the same thoughts.

Next day, at the end of the seventh period, I went to her class as usual without a reason or an excuse related to math.

"You will not believe what I will say, but I'm an expert in reading the minds my dear".

"Really?"
"Yes."

"How?"

"Easily. Mostly, I can figure it out all through the eyes; they show everything my dear." I answered.

"You're just kidding," she replied.

"Okay I will show you," I insisted,

"Just look at that student sitting there. She has troubles at home. Her parents seem tough with her. They force her to apply all the world's laws to make her later a perfect girl." "How are you saying that?" She interrupted.
"I can tell from her eyes. She obeys because of fear of the consequences. Well, look at the boy there.
He is so girly; his father is certainly like that with his wife. He doesn't know what she really needs. So, he pleases her by material things, as a role model not knowing that his boy is looking at him as his idol. Look, you can notice that from his eyes. He is trying to please others in order to earn the respect of his friends. He must have learned that at home from his father's life.

Look at the other girl there.
She is so spoiled and phony at the same time. That means her parents pretend love to each other; however that they're facing marriage problems. So they are trying on managing to live together. Thus they do everything for their daughter without meeting her emotional needs.
You can feel that she has emotional deprivation, as if she is searching for the parental love she craves for since her birth among the people around."

"Stop.", she said.
"Don't you believe me?" I asked.

She didn't say anything.
"Answer me, it seems you're not convinced by what I said", I repeated while standing beside her desk she was sitting on.

"Tell me about me", with a low voice she said, then continued,

"What have you figured out about me.?"

I was surprised by her question but smiled as an answer for her question.

"What?" she asked again.

I smiled again and stepped to the side as if I wanted to leave the room.

"It seems you saw nothing, or else you're not bold enough to speak", she meanly said it.

"It's not like that my dear," I answered, "but I respect your privacy."

But she insisted, "You said you read minds."

"Yes, I do." I answered now with a low voice.

"Then tell me anything about me."

I didn't have the guts to answer, but I tried to make fun of her question.

"Well, you are thinking of being naughty with me," I answered as I tried to move outside.

"Stop joking and for the last time, I ask you to tell me what you are reading in my eyes," she asked but this time with a serious and mean smile.

Well, I didn't say anything, but stepped forward so close to her, then caught her pen and wrote on a paper on her desk,

"You are not satisfied" then I kept on staring in her eyes with the same smile, stepped back, and off I went to the playground.

"What have I done?" I asked myself.

"She will misunderstand me; I really didn't mean to hurt her, but just answered what I saw after she insisted.

God, please forgive me if I crossed the limits, but really I don't want to lose a dear person like her."

"Dear, you crossed your limits by your impolite comment. Goodbye," was the message she texted me while I was walking in the school, feeling down about the unpardonable sin I committed.

"To hell with your goodbye", I replied by another text message and ran to her class.

"I didn't mean or intend to hurt you, but you insisted and I answered what I felt and saw in your eyes. It's not a polite way to deal with friends." I said toughly with an intention not to lose her.

"It's okay. It's okay," she repeated,
"Just leave me now; I'm really disturbed and I should leave", she said sadly while leaving.

My heart was broken into pieces, I couldn't say anything while watching her leave.

She was married, and later I got to know that she was facing problems with her husband similar to the ones I had previously.

We had a lot in common, but there were some differences especially in the way each of us faced our own life decisions.

Well, even though I listened to others' supportive opinions, it was always my decision which I took to face life.

I could see from her that she was an innocent person who couldn't make her own decisions. Instead she trusted and obeyed the words of the people closest to her. She always took their decisions into consideration, but didn't think of herself.

She reminded me of a princess called Isolde who was the heroine of the movie 'Tristan & Isolde'. They looked similar and shared many characteristics, especially in obeying the family's orders for the sake of their personal lives. She was able to sacrifice anything, even if it cost her to put any parental or friendly decision as a priority at the expense of herself. The same way she had in her marriage.

. The dissatisfaction was clear to see in her eyes, especially in their wedding photo album displayed on her husband's Facebook. She chose not to share these photos herself, which was even more telling of her misery.

The confession about what I read in her eyes was enough to call her Isolde for all the days to come.

I went back home and thought about the reason for her dissatisfaction. I figured out that her innocent and obedient character must have stemmed from childhood, allowing her to later be more aware of understanding and evaluating that her truthful heart needs to prioritise.

Even if she was married, there were white pigeons meant for her, as she thought about them as signs from God too.

"You're a donkey", she said on the second day after she invited me to sit with her on the porch of the teacher's room.

"What's the reason?" I asked.

"Don't argue, you are like that. I can read it in your eyes as you do in others."

I couldn't answer. I smiled and considered that nothing happened the day before. We continued on feeding our bodies with vitamin D from the sun while being content in each other's company.

Later, she started to bring along her baby daughter and allowed me to hold and play with her as if she were my own.

She even bought me sweets, and made me behave like a small child who waited for them every day.

She was perfectly nourishing my thirst.

"I'm leaving now, my dear. It's Thursday and I must go home to prepare some stuff before going to Inter-Continental Hotel at night," she said.

"Hey dear," I replied "Do you know what am I going to do this weekend?"

Standing behind the school's door in a hurry to move, her senses focused on my words,

"What?" she questioned me hurriedly before she left.

Smiling, I answered,

"I'm going to think about you. My dear."

And as usual, I went back home to my misery, this time smiling while thinking about her as a lovely candle lighting a little of my darkness.

Those days touched me deep inside my inner self. Her eyes became the target that my eyes wanted more than anything else.

That (Mwah) beside her name started to appear more and more on my phone for reasons such as missing some stuff in the teaching syllabus.

I came to her class many times to check fake papers in front of the supervisor, but as usual, just to say hi every moment either of us had the chance to. As days elapsed, we sat together more and we got along well.

"Hey dear, I'm free on the fourth period, if you have anything to do, just come and we will do it together," she called me.

"No worries dear, I will come," I answered.

"Dear it's the fifth period, come, I'm free now", she said on another day.

"I'm free too dear, but I'm sitting with some teachers in the second building. Give me five minutes and I will be there." I replied.

"Dear, I'm free at the third period, try to come; I'm alone on the desk by the restrooms. We must prepare a test for the students." She suggested.

"Okay, I'll finish and come. Should I bring my teacher's edition book with me?"

"It's okay; we don't need it because we already know the lessons."

We continued like that over the following weeks. Later, one or two hours were enough to remove the privacy between us through daily calls. We chatted about important and mundane events.

She was so warm hearted, so tender and such a helpful girl. She even didn't allow me to call her because she was afraid that I would spend the money I needed on her.

She noticed that I would get extremely cross and angry at the silly things some of my students would do.

She was kind enough to give me methods to communicate with those students, some of which had special needs who required more patience.

She didn't show any ego in her words, she just says,

"Take the advice from a dear person to a dear person like you."

I was about to hold her hand in order to thank her for being supportive of me.

I didn't care for work because I knew it was not where I belonged. It was a place to regain hope and to accept the Lord's will by trying to adapt to my new status quo, until God gives me another opportunity.

I began to feel as though that girl was touching me deep in the heart. My life was again meaningful with her jokes that meant so much to me.

She was truly filling my void with a feeling of happiness which I thought I would never experience again.

My health soon became better and I started to walk fast again.

I finally showed my students what I was keeping secret from them, my amazing and unexpected football skills. Most of the other teachers avoided joining any match when I was playing.

The obsession of my sickness started to fade away and passion kicked into my life and got stronger when I entered the school.

I wanted to call Mr. Sam to tell him about my life's changes.

Those changes were connected with someone special who gave me hope again, and helped me cruise well out from the valley of darkness.

I went up to the roof - the place in which I used to sit alone to pray for God.

I grabbed the phone to call the doctor, but I felt shameful because of my previous mean attitude. Also I felt that he was going to ask me details about the married Isolde and feared that he could recommend I stop any contact with her for a specific reason in his philosophic ideal world.

I looked at the sky, confused about what to do. I noticed that the moon was a crescent. Then, all of a sudden, the phone rang and answered all my worries.

"Hi, am I disturbing you from anything, dear?"

Isolde was on the phone.

"Nope, I was just watching the moon from the roof of my house." I answered, neglecting my real inner intentions.

"It seems incomplete, and less than half of its quarter is lit. Have a look at that little light inside, it looks like a smile".

"Please check it dear, it looks as if the moon is happy even when it's still partially loomed." I said as if asking her indirectly to share with me what I wanted to say to Mr. Sam.

"Maybe the best smile is the one that we have in our dark times." She interrupted as if reading my inner self, then said, "We all have dark times, but we can pass them by focusing on the bright times which would make us happy again."

Then, she insisted for me not to forget about the parent-teacher Conference held in the school on the next coming evening.

As soon as I hung up the call, I completely forgot about the idea of calling Mr. Sam. I took off the bracelet from my wrist and hid it in a safe place in the roof. It seemed pitch black compared to the amazing and bright idea that I focused on- The first parent-teacher conference.

Chapter14

"First Parent-Teacher Conference"

All parent-teacher conferences came with an unforgettable feeling. They were the break times of hiding our true feelings. They were the times of confessions and the time of the truth. It was simply our freedom as if both had confessed everything to each other.

I couldn't hide my feelings, and I was bold enough to express some of them. Every time she came, she was much brighter than the time before.

She took her freedom too and showed the true angel hidden under the school's uniform.

Frankly, the first parent-teacher meeting was the most unforgettable. Our eyes turned towards each other even when we chatted with the parents. She watched me well while smiling to every mother as I watched her carefully and saw every man who smiled at her.

I was looking at her with no limits. My heart was swirling with warm feelings that appeared on my face.

We were both discovering each other secretly but taking a break with a smile and direct eye contact every time the parents changed.

I'm sure the parents were happy when we told them in a high voice.

"I love your kid," she said.
"She is amazing and I'm happy with her behaviour," I was saying loudly too.

Those words were the same repeated answers for all the parents whether their kid was really good or bad.

But who cares, our confessions succeeded after they used to partially fail during school days.

That parent-teacher's meeting was the first day I attend with no bracelet in my hand, and it was clearly noticed with a smile from the lovely Isolde.

All the other parent-teacher's meeting were always compared to the first one as if it was the reference point somehow entitled- (The Confession Day).

Chapter 15

"Lovely Work Days"

"Then days went, work was a routine, but our feelings were getting more passionate; hide and seek was at its end."

Our eyes could show everything, and soon we got addicted to each other. Really, I don't remember that either of us were absent when we were both able to finish our sessions.

Events repeated themselves unlike our emotional potentials.

"Dear I'm having break." was what she started to say.
"On the fourth period, I think", I interrupted.

Then, "Dear I have a break on the…"
"Fifth period I also have, my dear", I interrupted again on the second day.
"Dear I'm free…"
"I know." I said, in a similar interruption I did every day. She noticed that I memorized her schedule.
"Dear…"
"Before speaking", I interrupted, "I'm free on the third period too, my dear, but try not to be late, because you

know that we must prepare a test." She was deeply astonished; "and don't forget to bring the teacher's edition because some teachers would be sitting with us on that table by the restrooms."

I felt her smile while I was saying those words on the phone from the other building.

She started to be confident of the idea that she is not fighting alone with her feelings.

"Yippie. It's Thursday my dear"
"I'm going to do the same as usual"
She said similarly behind the school's door.

But the answer of my same question was not the same:
"Do you know what I'm going to do this weekend?"

She blushed as she was rushing to her car when she heard my phrase. Her sunglasses hid the bright glean in her eyes.

"I'm going to miss you. My dear".

Then, I went back to my misery, but this time with a candle glowing brightly in the darkness.

Days were passing quickly and we continued to sit more with one another.

That girl impressed me with her morals and ethics. She used to tell me about herself and how that after she would get to know sweet people she would get addicted to them. She fears them leaving her because she can't forget anything they leave behind from imprints inside her, even their words, their smiles, their perfume, their gifts, the places they used to meet at, and the movies and songs they saw and listened to with each other.

And in case they hurt her, she will feel sorry for them, then forgive and love them again wishing that they could come back to their goodness.

Her words touched me deep inside, as if she was translating what the Lord said when he spoke about loving even our enemies.

Her words made me sure that whoever shares the same inner feelings with another is always connected by a secret power to meet even in a phony and materialistic society.

I was pretty sure that if this girl hurts me later, her words, beliefs and the innocence moulded in her will never allow me to forget or leave a pure-hearted person like her.

I fell in love with my mother's sweet-hearted character but would call her a weak person who can't ever defend herself in a society of hooligans.

Before, I was really tough with my mother. At times power was my only title. I was aware that my previous aggressive character relied on power like that of the jungle's law.

Getting along with the new atmosphere seemed the right way, and noticed that God helped me with that girl. She shared a similar experience, belief and attitude with me. We were both on the same frequency and the right track.

Those events made me think more and more about the pigeons I saw in my country from the balcony, and thought more about the letter M formed in their arrangement. I concentrated more on the image of the white pigeon showing.

"Was that image a vision for me, telling me to seek my own inner peace outside my country?

If yes, then why was the white pigeon showing clearly in that image?

Was it representing someone?" I wondered.

I wondered if it was a message from God for a new and peaceful life to be shared with a girl who looked and acted perfectly like a white pigeon, the same as the white pigeon that was showing clearly in the pigeons' arrangement.

I realized that she really behaves and looks like a white pigeon that was so peaceful, so innocent. Then flew away when it was afraid.

Those really were her characteristics; she used to face others with the love and peace of good intention for all others. When she faced an embarrassing situation, silence was her response as if exaggerating that fear and she flew away as a pigeon does.

She was not like anyone around her, even in her skin colour, where all used to call her "Snow White" because of her unusually smooth and white skin.

She was the whitest person I'd ever seen.

Thinking was my favourite hobby. I thought more about what I wanted. I had never been in such a situation, I always used to love girls with eagle's characteristics who were strong enough to face and take their rights in similar cases.

"A Queen should always have some traits of a King in order to rule a Kingdom together", was my previous belief.

I never loved to be with peaceful girls who faced challenges with a smile like my mother, who was always blamed for her sweet-hearted nature towards all of society.

But after meeting her, I started to believe that a girl with a pigeon's characteristics isn't bad at all.

I noticed that when God spoke about the human's inner peace. He chose a white pigeon from all his creatures to carry the olive twig as a symbol of peace.

Once again, I wondered,

"What am I doing?

God, is it fair for me to consider this girl as a gift sent from you to help me apply your words?

Shall I apply your words by opening a door for a peaceful love to help me?

Or is it the truth of failing at your trials by avoiding my responsibility toward my promises and ignoring your words which call for staying away from other men's women- a married woman who is not my spiritual right?

Is that really me?
Am I a betrayer?

Even if I live alone in my own darkness, I must stop that new light from reaching me and continue the search for someone else as I promised myself."

I was really confused and seemed to ignore everything I believed in just to have tentative relief instead.

Even if I was in a far place, away from anyone who knew me before, those ideas kept following me.

"Dear, you must always remember that the Lord is with us and he will always enlighten our path if we obeyed and trusted his words", I said those words from the roof of my home using the phone to whom I used to call Isolde.

But the answer I heard was:

"Dear, why are you saying those things?"

"I know them, and I really don't want to hear them, I just want you to know the following:

You are a sweet person.
You are a person of pure heart.
You are really a sweetheart.

And whatever happens between us, remember what I'm telling you for the rest of your life.

You are a light-hearted person" she repeated.

Chapter 16

"The Up Rise of My Inner Struggle"

Speaking of my inner self, my heart was saying,

"Please, Mind. She is not doing anything wrong. As long as she is not saying any love words everything is still intact.

Please let me enjoy living as she is expressing her inner feelings to me. I feel alive again.

I've missed those words from someone who means them. It's really okay if you feel someone cares about you at times when you don't care about anything that's around, even about yourself."

My heart was encouraging me to continue my way while trying to convince my mind about his situation.

"Hey dear..." my mind answered.

"Please don't make a fool of me, as if I don't know you.

Well, everything you are saying is perfectly true. But I wonder if you can prove to me that you have no feelings toward her.

Dear, you are being a perfect betrayer, and as you always advise others, I advise you.

Remember that the Lord judges the heart- the source of temptations. He is watching everything closely, my dear."

"Remember well 'Heart', that God's words are always above everything."

My mind continued blaming me and enjoyed dominating my heart. My mind succeeded to take the lead with those words.

But through that struggle inside. I asked my inner self "What should I do...?"

"You know well what to do my dear," the answer was coming from my mind

"It needs courage to put limits to your heart, but shame on you, you're gaining strength only when you are being selfish. You are heedless to the words and laws of God."

Going up to the roof stopped being my place of peace. Instead, it became the main battlefield, and that's because most of the calls and struggles were done there.

"Say something...anything...just...say anything to me...aren't you feeling anything?" Isolde asked.

"Please... I'm begging you. Don't ask those questions again," I replied.

"Why?" She insisted.

"It's not something I can handle dear. Please try to understand".

"Understand what?" She repeated.

"Okay, I will try to explain, but I don't know how much you will understand me and my situation."

"Say anything sweetheart..." she said waiting to hear my words.

"Dear, what I say is always coming from inside. My inner has two leaders, and the words that come outside actually come from the one who dominates the other.

Those leader are my heart that always proved to be the stronger one, and my mind who has always served by organizing my heart's needs."

"So what?" She asked again.

"I'm going through hard times and my heart is sick, and consequently the mind is in control now, so he stood up against the heart's demands and is now the one in charge to lead my inner self in the name of God."

"What does that mean?" She asked again.

"It means that my mind is dominating and my heart is struggling. Hence, the mind won't allow any word to come out for the sake of God. Please understand dear." I answered.

"Oh, yes, I understand
You are a person who enjoys hurting me" was her answer to my confusing words.
"Honey please understand," I said.
"Please repeat the word honey another time." She replied.

"Dear... You don't know what you are doing to me," was my answer every time we were on the phone talking from the roof- the battlefield.

She really loved me, but she didn't ever know how I was living. She didn't give up. She fought strongly and did her best to stay in touch with the one she had true feelings for. I realized well that all the calls she did previously were not to help her in the daily duties as it was shown for me.

She was not calling to hear my words as much as to listen to my voice.

Stopping those calls was a hard decision, especially after she became a special person in my life. We avoided talking about the struggle which prevented me from acknowledging any of my feelings and continued talking about daily things as if we both surrendered to our feelings in a respectful way, in order not to show what our inner longed to admit.

Chapter 17

"May Fifth Again"

May the fifth came and I was alone remembering what happened to me on the same date in the past two years.

Robert's accident was the first event of that date which I was missing for the second time.

And the second event of that date was my admittance to the hospital. It was the reason I forgot to put the flowers on the grave of my dear Robert after he passed away the year before.

I went up to the roof to tell Isolde about my pain of that date and also to tell her that I could have been killed before knowing her on the same particular day.

I was excited about that call. I lay under the sky looking at that (Mwah) beside her name while having no answer.

I felt angry at her indifference, as if she belonged to me only.

"If you're not in a good mood, or very busy, you have no right not to answer my call", I wrote those mean words in a text message.

She called after just minutes from the bathroom, "How could you write those words to me, I was with my husband eating; can't you notice that I'm married, dear. Anyway, was it something urgent? Are you okay sweetheart?"

Her answer made me feel ashamed of my attitude and I had no strength to say that I needed her, but answered, "I was so uncomfortable from some problems happening to me especially when May the fifth arrives."

Chapter 18

"Final Parent-Teacher Conference"

It was the last parent-teacher meeting of the school year. She looked amazing, like a swan with a green dress and a shining necklace. She was a wonderful angel.

I turned the Bluetooth on my phone and took for her a cup of coffee and some sweets from the main room. I told her to do the same on her phone to read my Bluetooth messages.

We had the same phone brand. She answered, "I didn't notice that before and I'm really surprised to have this option in my lovely phone."

I sent her a silly song that described her smile, her lips and all her beauty. I looked straight into her eyes, and watched her smile and waited for a reply.

Even though the song was silly, she liked it because she felt that I really meant the lyrics of the song.

We were strongly connected together secretly before all other people as close colleagues.

I was totally another person, I was in complete charge of that lady. My heart was responding strongly in the presence of the mind who was almost damaged at every parent's meetings.

It was time to leave; she went out while I was still waiting to finish with some late parents.

I finished quickly and went fast outside to check if I can still see her.

Outdoors, I turned to the left to see her standing in the playground spending time talking with an ugly teacher just to catch me before she leaves.

She was waiting for me. By the time she finished her talk, I had reached her smiling secretly. Then we headed toward the fingerprint to sign out.   .

We moved silently; only heartbeats could be felt as we synchronized our paces.

Her car was parked by the administration,

With no self-control, I opened and jumped into the seat and closed the door while she smiled gently and opened her door.

I was hooked by her gracefulness. My heart pounded faster and faster as I gazed into her eyes.

"Would you want me to give you a ride home?" she asked.

"If you do that, you will never leave my home",

I answered with a true smile with fire up inside, I objected and remembered God's words to prevent myself from accepting her offer.

Then I continued, "Tomorrow we have school and I think you know what I will do till tomorrow comes." I asked, knowing already what her answer was. My heart was perfectly leading my inner.

She replied with a smile as I stepped outside the car and watched her drive away.

"You will miss me." She said as she passed the main gate.
"You're being smarter with time. That's really my girl" I hung up with her just before reaching her home.

Enrique Iglesias was our star of songs through the parent-teacher meeting.

Daily, in the subconscious, we thought, imagined and missed being with each other.

"Dear, I think it's not your break now. Why have you left your class? Why are you here in my class?" She asked me warmly.
"Why are you asking dear?" I replied.

With a shy smile, she answered happily, "Do you know that deep inside, I was calling you and thought of going to your class now to see you. I swear."

"Don't swear dear, because I sensed that you're calling me and came for the same reason." I said.

The school's graduation ceremony came, and I was supposed to see her, but the administration put us on different timings. She was in the morning while I was in the evening ceremony.

I had to tend a specific location. I had to stand and watch the guests. They didn't accept that I wanted to choose my own place to be. For an hour and a half, I was on the phone with my dear, careless about that ceremony. I cared less about the consequences of that.

I was indifferent to all the teachers and the principal who seemed mad at me.

As days passed, that girl proved to me that she never forgets anything. She asked me again about the main reason I was angry on the fifth of May.

"I'm truthful my dear, and I really respect the times that were check points in my life, I just wanted to share it with you."

I answered hiding my main inner reason.

She wasn't totally convinced by my answer, and later she mocked me by saying the word 'Truthful' in a funny way.

She made fun of me later when I was in a shopping centre with some friends. I laughed at myself for being unable to give her a better convincing answer other than the one I really mean. Then all of a sudden, the word 'Truthful' appeared printed on the packaging of blue boxers (men's underwear) with a smiley face next to it.

I couldn't hold myself from laughing at that coincidence. I told her that it was a sign from God to prove that I was really truthful in my previous answer.

I bought the underwear as I also bought her a music box as a gift from a dear and honest person.

On the phone I told her about my competition a year ago, and among the competitors, I had beaten the opponent who was representing her university. I was surprised when she told me that she was in the audience watching the championship. She sat in a safe place since she was pregnant and remembered my opponent who lost after being beaten wildly by an unknown and crazy person.

Before we ended the call, she told me that she was going to travel to our country on June 27th, which was three days before the school's summer vacation. Her reason was private, but she promised to tell me about it later. She said that time was going so fast, let's enjoy its best moments.

I came back home and went up to my roof. I wondered about why God was sending me those funny peaceful signs while I was exceeding the limits of his words.

My heart was tired of loneliness, and it was taking the lead heedless for the consequences.

I discovered that the mission I undertook to forget the past was about to fail; it was destroying me rather than mending my pieces together.

I felt upset at the weakness of my promise. It was unable to stop my heart asking God to give him the permission to love the white pigeon that gave him peace during all his battles.

This day was a checkpoint that I will talk about later to show how it gave my heart the courage to fight for its love as a dominant leader especially in (My Term Test).

Chapter 19

"My Term Test"

That lady was a smart teacher in testing the honesty of every word I said.

Saying the word "Truthful" was going to be tested one coming day, when I became like a student who was tested with quizzes to check how much he loved the subject.

There were no students attending the school, only teachers who were preparing the lessons for the second year.

Most of our time was free and the school became the perfect place to be on our reality.

Well, June 13th came and I went to the school without studying, like a student, the same way I used to be throughout my whole life. In that day, I was subjected to a sudden unprepared test, but this time it was a Term Exam.

She was so angry and totally nervous, she asked me toughly to stay in her class.

"Dear why are you speaking like that?" I asked; on that day, I was wearing a black shirt with blue jeans and that boxer with the word 'Truthful'. Also I was holding her sweet little baby girl while she was on the ground.

"Stay here," she said

But a friend of hers entered to see the baby girl as all other teachers used to do.

The baby girl stood up alone and she was still around eight months old.

"Look she is standing alone," I said with a surprised look on my face. Suddenly, the girl fell to the floor. The second teacher looked at me as if I had jinxed the girl.

I directly caught up my little doll and held her tightly to my chest. I was nervous after being disturbed by that silly and dumb teacher.

The teacher left the class. I looked again at my lady and asked her toughly,

"What's wrong?"

"Why are you acting crazily like that?"

She hushed me with a low voice and said,

"Close the door well and come sit beside me without saying anything, please."

I was perplexed, but I did what she said and closed the door, then sat beside her silently watching her moves.

"Give me your hand."
I did.

She held it, passed it to her heart, and held it up and kissed it. After a while, she asked me,

"Till when?"

"Till when what?" I replied sweating.

"Till when will we stay like this?
I can't continue on hiding my feelings.
You mean to me so much.
My dear.., you are so sweet
You are so wonderful.
I lose control when you're around.

You make me go crazy.

I'm in love with you dear.

Just answer me, till when will we stay like this?"

Here I will interrupt her talk to depict my inner monologue. My mind was worried about my possible answer and tried to do his best to prevent any reckless answer from addressing her, "I think you arrived to the point I warned you about previously.

You secretly opened the door, but now try to close Mr. Betrayer. Stop sweating and show me your respect to God's teachings"

My mind said those words as the last bullets before losing control.

"Go to hell." My 'heart' answered my 'mind'.

"Yes, I want to enjoy what God has endowed me with. That's what I deserve, and I'm happy to see her like me fighting for her love.

I will reciprocate that love. Remember well 'mind', you used to follow me and to obey my words. So manage what I want or go to hell."

Now back to me,

"Just find a place and I'm ready," I answered.

"How?" She asked.

"I don't know how, I just know a little in this country, but you can manage it," I said again.

"Maybe, it would be better to meet in our country," was her final answer before she heard my positive confirmation,

"It would be my pleasure sweetheart".

The Thirteenth of June was my successful term test.

That day, I heard what I didn't expect from her. She dared to confess her inner feelings, as I had no idea that my spontaneous response exceeded all of the redlines of God's words.

But above all, I loved the idea that I was finally going to be her student. I had always wanted to be since we first met.

I used to hate number thirteen, but after that day, it became an amazing number for me.

June the Thirteenth became a new main checkpoint in addition to the parent-teacher's meetings confession days that changed everything.

We stopped hiding our emotions but embodied them in words and acts in-between us.

Since then, coming to school became a daily rendezvous. I can't find the words to describe those lovely days- it was an outstanding period in my life.

On every rendezvous, she wore her best dresses.

All others noticed that we became more than close colleagues, but she didn't care.

Her eyes were glowing brightly and gave me no chance to read again the word (unsatisfied) that became meaningless during the days that we had together.

Chapter 20

"The Day Before Summer Vacation"

"It's June Twenty Sixth, a day before leaving to our country; don't waste our time. Just come up to the second floor in the KG department," she messaged me.

"I'm coming," I replied and rushed to see her.

I entered the class just to see her wearing an appealing short dress. I held back my compliment in front of the teachers who were playing with her daughter.

I smiled and waited for the teachers to go away, then said,

"Your dress looks like a cleaning uniform."

"What?" She was anticipating another sweet compliment.

"That's a brand, can't you see? Or the cleaner girls are the ones who appeal to you?"

"I don't care about brands as much as I do for janitors, especially if you were one of them working in my house," I answered with a naughty smile and repeated slowly, " I truly wish for that, my dear."

She was excited by the compliment. Later we resumed our day as we casually did before.

At the end of the day, I told her that I changed my flight schedule just to travel with her on the same airplane.

She couldn't believe my words and her eyes especially when I gave her the music box which profoundly touched her. She hugged me secretly before we could get busted by anyone.

Chapter 21

"The Missing Part"

I came back home feeling exhilarated about my new refreshing life. The idea of darkness no longer existed. I felt relieved from any self-responsibility related to saints. I stopped watching for signs that could get my attention to the words of God

Every warrior deserves a rest, and I couldn't believe that I finally had it.

I thought only about traveling to my country. I imagined the time when I would meet Isolde alone.

It was more than a dream. It was like living in heaven while thinking and living those moments with her.

I couldn't wait for the next day and called her just to hear her voice from the roof that became at last, the place of romantic calls.

We spoke as usual for around two hours. During the call, I noticed the moon was fully bright and told her to check it, it was as if the moon was finally satisfied after it was looking like a smile.

We ended the call with no intention to hang up. I came back down to prepare my bag.

As I was packing up, I recalled some memories about my country and discovered that I still missed something important. My hand was empty and the bracelet was still on the roof. I ran back up the roof to bring it down again. I arrived in the secret place in which it was hidden, then tried to fetch it.

But suddenly, it disappeared and everything turned black. My heartbeats rose dramatically. I fell on the ground and almost choked as I ran out of breath.

Unfortunately, I realized that I was losing my consciousness.

I lay on the ground like a dead person on the roof.

I stayed out for half an hour to be awakened by my ringing phone.

"What are you doing?"

"I called you many times," it was my brother calling from my country.

"Tell me brother, is there anything wrong?" I could barely answer.

"Mother was admitted to the hospital an hour ago, and the doctors are confused about the unknown reason of her sickness.

If you can, try to come by tomorrow. She really needs you beside her, brother."

I was terrified to hear those words and tried hard to say,

"Tomorrow evening, I will be back, brother."

I picked up the charm and looked all over the roof that became my cheating den. Then went back to my inner conflicts.

Chapter 22

"The Obligatory Yet Saving Decision"

All my heart's desires were in shock. I recognized well that I had crossed the red limits and swayed away from all of God's teachings. I officially became a perfect traitor.

I became afraid of traveling back to my country in fear of shame, of lying, and of failure in what I had promised myself.

A huge war with no weapons was about to wage in the next day.

Being truthful was my only weapon, but faded by a forbidden relationship with a white pigeon, where all the events in the relationship became evidence in the hands of my mind who ordered me to stop everything in the name of God.

"It seems you only remember God when you are weak," my mind preached me.

"Is that what the word 'Truthful' means for you Mr. Betrayer?"

With a feeling of worry, I urgently asked for help to assure victory before officially starting my war.

But the answer was, "This question has no answer now. The war is about to start without any clear idea of how to confront it. I have no idea if victory could even exist because your disgrace of God's words left us with no weapons to withstand the coming long war.

We are now fighting just to restore your condition to the time when you came to Dubai.

Death is much easier than losing that war."

My mind was winning and my heart was frightened from the pending events. He kept silent as he obeyed any order that could cure the damage he had caused so far.

"Mind answer me, what should I do?" I asked sadly.

But instead, he requested,

"Forget about me and the heart, just imagine the time when you arrive to your country.

How can you smile at your mother who is about to pass away because of your indifference to God's words?

How can you forgive yourself if anything happened to her?

How can you look into her eyes when you are eating the 'Forbidden Fruits'?

Where may you put your eyes if you thought to face her and all about your forbidden betraying relation?

Can you then be yourself?

Can you ask for help from God?

I really cannot understand how you can pray before going to sleep every night?

I don't know how you even evaluate yourself after giving a promise to the Lord and failing to keep it.

You travelled abroad to cure yourself under the shelter of his words and now you're coming back to your country to continue the treason you started here.

Just imagine how you would stand before God when you laughed at his words.

Mr. Sam was right about his comments, but your ego is a small part of your truth.

I don't have any idea about what's going to happen later, but you still have the choice either to stop or to continue your betrayal."

The scolding continued, "I can't understand how you couldn't stop a relationship while knowing that your sickness might end your life in a second.

Are you able to marry that girl if she got divorced?

Do you have the courage to face a back-stabbed husband?

How can you destroy her life and then desert her for the same reason you deserted Robina?

Everything you planned to be honest about again was destroyed and became the reason to destroy your beloved ones, as your mother once told you.

I don't understand how you have forgotten all of those facts and followed your stupid heart.

A year ago you left your country as a weak creature but with the intention to reconstruct yourself in the right way; however, you became weaker than ever and earned the title 'Traitor' instead of;

'Truthful'

I told you those words from the beginning, but you didn't care about words that were said before the presence of God almighty.

I don't have any single idea about what's going to happen later. A black cloud is blinding me. Nevertheless, the choice is yours whether to stop or to continue your wicked betrayal."

Those words were killing me deep inside and the feeling of guilt overwhelmed me.

"My dear…" I heard again the words coming from the same source, but they sounded defeated. My mind continued addressing me, but now with a real worry that would only survive if I were to change my ways.

"My dear, we need weapons. Weapons that would only keep your mother alive after being sick by a reason that you only know".

"Those weapons need to be ready by tomorrow, precisely at the time you arrive your country.

Your country that became the only place to forget about your betrayal you committed in Dubai.

Being truthful is your only weapon to face everything, and I think, you know exactly how to restore it."

My mind finished his conversation, waiting for me to realize that ending my latest peaceful relation was the only way to survive the pending and miserable unknown.

I walked down to my home wearing my charm with a resolution to finish everything. But deep inside, I was only focusing on a sentence Isolde once told me while I was asking her about the reasons for her problematic marriage.

All of our memories flashed before my eyes. My mind was searching strongly to find any memory that could help avoid a clash with the blind heart during my meeting with Isolde in the day after.

"I'm a queen my dear. A queen, but living imprisoned in her kingdom."

It was a sentence my mind remembered to show my broken heart that Isolde was mistaken in loving a prince to save her from her misery. In fact he was unable to save himself from his worst nightmare that haunted him day and night within his destroyed state.

That sentence bitterly encouraged me to think about confessing to her my secret before arriving in my country.

Chapter 23

"Shock Day"

The last day came and she was wearing a lovely black dress as if she was giving her condolences for the death of our relationship.

"My dear, I want to tell you something important, but first I want you to promise to understand me," I said gently.

"What's going on dear?" she asked.

"My dear, we are going to our country today, but you don't know what will happen to me there.
My life is getting complicated and hardship is surrounding me from all angles.
Believe me, death is much easier than facing myself, and I really crossed the limits in our relationship."

"You are..."
(My Broken Angel) my heart tried to interfere, but, "You are a dear person who helped me a lot", was what she heard me saying.
"And the only solution is," I continued shaking, "to stop everything and finish what we started by the time we arrive in our country".

I could barely maintain composure, but I gazed into her eyes so as not to miss a single moment in our last day before saying goodbye for good.

"Today we will travel and it will be our last day my dear," I said. Then repeated, "I really want you to understand my situation, I know what I'm doing. But I'm just trying my best to be responsible of my words, and I beg you to believe that I really didn't intend to hurt you."

"Just forgive me sweetheart; forgive me for everything I said especially these words. I'm sure a day will come and you will realize what I was passing through."

"You were my only candle that brightened my darkness.

You really gave me peace in time of wars. My wars will never end, and now I shall go back to face them alone, my dear.

I'm really sorry, Maria Bella."

I didn't know why I called "Isolde" by her real name for the first time, as if the truth was crystal clear.

She was totally shocked.

She didn't believe that I could be the one saying those words.

She tried to concentrate well on my lips to check if it really was me who was speaking.

She kept silent while I was speaking. I saw her eyes looking clearly at the bracelet in my hand. Then with a sad smile, she surrendered to my hard decision and showed respect by saying,

"I will tell you what to bring for her.

She must have the best gift from a lovely and adorable person like you, my dear."

Her innocent response stabbed me in the heart.

"A teddy bear...?

A teddy bear is the best gift, sweetheart" she repeated as if it's the last time she will say that.

"She will surely love it. Believe me, that's what I'd want from my beloved."

"I will look for teddy bears in the Duty free area before I see you on our flight, my dear," I replied hoarsely.

I went to the administration and surprised them too by my resignation.

It was horrible, just like an inmate waiting the death penalty.

I went back home and couldn't stay in my apartment.

I took my friend's car and drove away with the excuse of shopping but as a matter of fact, it was to forget what I had experienced in that terrible day.

Chapter24

"The Farewell Trip"

I went to the airport early pretending to enjoy traveling to my country after a long year of work.

I made my last call with her to ask about her full name to book her a seat beside mine. Then I went to the Duty Free to buy a gift which she thought I was taking to my beloved girl. Letting her believe that was the perfect answer to leave each other forever.

I was a little late to go the waiting area since I was confused which gift to get for 'Mother'.

I finally arrived at the waiting area to see Maria Bella still in her black dress as if giving the perfect look for the goodbye trip.

She was waiting for me. Her eyes were staring angrily showing me the blame of wasting our last moments.

She nervously continued looking at my hands and thought that the teddy bear was the cause of my late arrival.

I noticed how dearly she wanted to get rid of the bag in which the gift was, but refrained as if God saved my laptop which was in there too. However, the gift was in my hand bag.

We boarded the airplane and took our seats. I sat by the window. We arranged our stuff, put on the seatbelts, and prepared ourselves for the take-off.

In that moment she told me, "Your flight was on the 30th of June, but you said that you changed it for me,"

"So what?" I replied.

"This means that you are flying in my airplane and you should respect my feelings and share with me unforgettable memories till we arrive to our country's airport."

I smiled back and told her," I'm always like that when I'm with you, but as you said, till we arrive to our airport, my dear"

As the plane started moving, the Christ's name was what I heard from her lips after she crossed and kissed her hand then gave it to me for kissing for the sake of praying for a safe trip. But then, she kissed the back of her hand as a sign of love which I pretended that I didn't know its symbolism. I smiled back to her in appreciation.

I was looking at Dubai from the plane and searched for the school. The plane ascended and I was insistent that I would find it.

The plane started to take and I smiled, it was my favourite part of the flight, to me it meant a new start that with the strength and power to fly again.

I continued looking and finally saw the school from my seat. I turned to ask her to watch our love nest from above as a start for our goodbye trip, but unfortunately, she was unable to join me because she was closing her eyes and praying. I respected her prayers and closed my eyes too, then asked God to be with us and bless our souls wherever we are and to forgive our mistakes.

I felt warmth on my hand. I realized that it was her hand catching mine, but I kept closing my eyes. I understood that she was afraid and was trying to feel safe with someone who deeply felt her inner desires.

The plane soared up until it reached the required level. The crew started to bring the food. She was holding her baby, then handed her to me, as I did while taking the food.

Then, she uttered,

"What was the colour of the teddy bear you bought your beloved girl?"

"Black", I answered strictly.

"How come?"

"Yes, black", I repeated in the same way.

"You're joking…"

"No, I'm not."

"Yes you are, no one brings his beloved girl a black teddy bear."

"Yes, I do, and believe me, she will love its smell." I answered again.

"Why are you talking about its smell?" she asked confused.

"It's a perfume, silly. I bought her a perfume in a black case not a teddy bear." I insinuated.

She didn't say anything. She reassured herself regarding my acts. She understood some of my inner wars by a smile. She certainly could feel my love to her, but for some unknown reason, I kept it inside.

"Can I have more cheese please, and a piece of bread?" I asked the flight attendant.

She handed the cheese to me, but I told her that I want to have more for the baby and for myself.

She taught me the etiquette of arranging the eating utensils, but the small baby ruined everything. The bread and cheese was spread on our faces, instead.

I asked for more cheese as if I suffered from hunger. Here she said,

"That blond host is so sweet; he is really lovely and I want to give him a flying kiss." She tried to tease me.

"You can shut up, my dear, and give him what you want later - not when you are with me." was my answer then continued kissing the small baby when it was my turn to put her on my lap.

Some people that we knew in Dubai, were also with us on the same plane, and used to take the small baby in turn. We realized that they never stopped sneaking ... looks at us through all the trip.

But, we didn't mind. We continued our talks, shared our memories, and wondered about how we would miss each other.

We were truly in harmony. We tried to enjoy the last moments that passed incredibly swiftly. We didn't feel the time. It travelled faster than the airplane itself.

They really were the best moments we ever spent together. We looked and touched each other secretly and boldly. We read each other's minds; she became a good reader after that year. She finally realized well that we can take hard decisions to survive, but our eyes always speak everything about the internal feelings especially the moments that satisfy us.

The plane started descending and we prepared for landing. I wanted to tell her about my sickness in order to confess what I was still hiding before leaving her.

Before that, I wanted to know more about the weird things that made her marriage faulty. It was more than marriage problems. I always had this feeling and linked her secret of traveling alone on June 27th to what I felt.

"You still didn't tell me about the reason behind flying early to our country. You promised to confess it." I said with a sad smile as I got prepared to be tough as our arrival was close.

"I promised to confess when our feelings were honest, but now everything has changed and the promise became meaningless. I prefer to keep it as a secret between me and my Lord."

Her words were enough to stop any comment. I clearly understood that her little secret could be a catalyst that might reconcile her with God's words.

I kept silent and turned to have a look outside at my country as the plane descended slowly.

Suddenly, the view became black. My nerves ached as I started to lose control and suffered shortness of breaths.

My brain was blocked and the veins of my head were about to explode. I couldn't to see anything around me. My heartbeats were unstable. They beat fast to a level that left me unable to move. Waiting for my soul to leave my body was my only response.

I asked God for help. No one from the cabin crew was able to help because they were all in their seats ready for landing.

I was really dying, but suddenly, I realized that the Lord was responding to my prayers when I felt Maria Bella's hands massaging my head without even asking her.

I thought that God was trying to save me from all my miseries and misfortunes. He was just giving me a happy ending by resting in peace in the hands of the person whom I loved but had no right to.

Soon after caressing my head softy, I restored my composure, but my heartbeats were still high. I thanked God for I was still alive. The plane landed safely. Surprisingly, Maria Bella got to know the secret about my dangerous sickness.

Chapter 25

"Arriving to My Country's Airport"

"When the doors open, new life will start. Everyone will go their separate ways. We will forget everything; we will not look at each other or say any word. We will just walk out as strangers. Okay dear?" I said.

"Okay my dear," she agreed.

With no other words to say, we arrived to the airport's doors. We walked down the aisle to pick our luggage. It was the fastest flight we'd ever had.

I kissed the baby girl whom I considered as my child and looked at her mother for the last time.

The doors of the airport opened, we walked silently and looked to see our parents from the crowds waiting outside.

No voice was there, we continued watching each other without showing it.

We continued walking, thinking of our similar dark unknown.

"Honey, there you are"

"Sister, you are being more beautiful than ever.

The baby is so cute".

Her parents were shouting happily and kissing the baby after they picked her up from her mother's hands, as I used to do.

I watched them secretly while I was hugging my brother.

I hugged my brother warmly and tried to focus on him and my friend. I tried my best not to turn or say a single word. I even tried not to say goodbye as we promised before the doors opened.

My friend hugged me and looked me up and down, as did my brother. I smiled as if I was in another world away from reality, not as they expected. I turned back to see her doing the same, gazing at me while smiling back at her family as I was doing with mine.

"Oh Lord, my heart breaks apart when I recall those moments."

I looked forward and asked my brother and friend to bring the car. I tried to control myself in that agonizing situation. However, they were thrilled to know who the girl was that I was looking at as passionately.

I kept silent as a child just like Maria Bella used to do when she had no answer to a question.

"Just bring the car brother, I'm really feeling tired. I was very ill before arriving at the airport." I told them in a way to explain why I wasn't in a proper shape.

We moved outdoors with my luggage, but now I was out of the system- out of order- I was totally losing control.

My heart throbbed with passion; I could not compare it to any other feeling.

I looked around frantically to check if I could still have the chance to see her. My brother was in the parking lot and I was so nervous.

I just wanted to see her one more time.
I just wanted to say goodbye another time.

I turned around in all directions, then looked up to the sky asking my Lord to respond.

I looked back at the parking only to see her alone looking at me secretly. With a broken smile, she waved her hand at me. That moment was overwhelming.

As she moved to her sister's car, I ran up fast and left my bags on the ground. I shouted for my brother to bring his car quickly.

I arrived up to hear the horn of my brother's car down beside the bags.

I turned back to see her moving away with her family to the unknown .In that moment I wanted to join her in seeking the unknown, too.

I came back down nervously asking my brother again why they were late, but with a sarcastic laugh, they said, "Be patient bro, the parking was full and we were trying to come quickly,"

I didn't know what to say after they said, "Calm down Champ; we don't want to get beaten by your power gained abroad. We didn't know that the recharged powers makes a person in such a hurry."

They killed me with those words. They didn't know that my rush was for the passion of my official suicide that could have been such a disaster to my past commitments.

We hit the road with no words to say. They felt something was wrong, but I repeated and explained that I had a migraine in the plane from the change in atmospheric pressure, and I was just waiting to sleep.

I arrived home calmly as if I was in a funeral, I sat with whom I'd missed, but I was absent-minded thinking of what happened in the airport.

"My mind... my heart... my principles; all were confused.

But my mind was still trying to keep the lead.

My dear, just go back to the moment before the airport doors opened and remember well your words. Don't think except what you promised, and remember well, that you have a sick mother waiting for you here.

"Try to be loyal my dear, just be yourself- the truthful one. I know that you are still truthful." My mind again reminded me about my persistence in following my words till death as if it was really the only way to survive.

Chapter 26

"My War's First Night"

It was midnight and everyone was asleep, but I was still awake; still in shock of what had happened.

I couldn't sleep. I came back to my country to open a new page of a truthful life. My heart was obeying my mind's words to cope with the war, but when the doors of the airport opened, my heart cheated and tried to open his own new white page.

I closed my eyes, and tried to hug my pillow that looked as white as the one who grabbed hold of my heart.

At that point, I gave in to my heart's desires.

"I can't be fake, I cannot avoid that forbidden feeling. Is it a new life?

Is it another door?

Is it another sign from God to inform that I can start a life with a new love?

Or it is a tricky war that will be merciless for both?

What a test Lord." I repeated, then listened again to my inner voices,

"Stop your lethal thoughts and retreat. Go back to behind the airport's doors, my dear." My mind was saying.

"It's a destructive war…blackness is everywhere. Please, go back behind the airport's doors and stay there my dear". Then my 'heart' interrupted, violating the truce with my mind that was done days before.

"It's okay my friend, you know of all the times I've suffered when you took the decision to desert Robina. I've been thirsty for so long. I was feeding only from God's words indifferent to my craving. I lost my beloved ones. I became spiritless for so long, and if you want to go back to the airport's doors, go to the time when they were opened and remember well that a chance of a new life was given to me, as if I was born again. It wasn't in my hands. My beats raced because of love not pain. I'm sick enough of pain, dear. I really want to live that peace again, whatever is the cost. I want to live what I felt after the doors opened", my heart continued fighting, with no mercy for his rights that he truly felt.

I thought about whom I called Isolde.
"Is she feeling the same?
Is she remembering and living what happened after the doors opened?
Or has she gone back to our words before the doors opened?
What is she doing now?
Is she happy again?
Please, God help me.
I'm heartbroken."

As my inner-self questions kept showering down my head, the phone rang.

I picked it up quickly and checked that I was not dreaming.

She was the one calling…
"Honey…honey…honey…
I missed you, I missed you like never before.

I couldn't call you all night because my family had prepared a party for me, but I'm not thinking of anything except you.

I went to the balcony secretly to speak with you.
I missed you honey. I want to be with you and only with you sweetheart. Please, I want to see you my love."

I answered and my tears filled my eyes after I heard her crying while saying those words.

"I was waiting for you, Maria Bella.
I told them all to sleep because I was tired, but couldn't close my eyes because you were on my mind.
I was asking God to tell me anything about you.
You really took over my heart, and made it beat again.
I was going to follow you, but you left the airport quickly.
Thank God that no one noticed that we were so attached to each other.
Maybe that was a message from God to remind us that everything we had was not righteous.

I missed you more than ever, but this feeling should not proceed. Everything we planned for was destroyed in the airport; we shall keep our promise."

"What are you saying?" she interrupted. "It was a proof for our true love.
Please don't break my only happy moments that I still have. Just be credible with your feelings, listen to your heart, honey.
Your heart that was one with mine in that airport.
Please sweetheart, don't leave me alone, and just give our love another chance."
She broke my heart as she was weeping on the phone.

"How can I be truthful by correcting the mistake I did with another betrayal?

You are a married woman with a beautiful kid. Even if you were single, by knowing my secret should be enough for you to understand my situation. It was the same reason why I broke up with a former girlfriend.

I'm sick my dear, I'm not able to do anything, except to prepare myself to die sooner or later.

Please, sweetheart, all the circumstances show that I'm not the right person and it was not meant for us to be together.

I should have recognized that earlier and must have accepted your first goodbye message that you sent me rather than yielding to God's punishment as a painful message to leave you now."

But she continued, "I love you, with all my senses and I don't care about your sickness.

I will help you to cure yourself. Please understand my love. I beg you to stay with me. I need you more than ever. We can start again from that airport" she repeated.

"What happened in the airport was meant to end at that airport." I interrupted.

"Please dear, I don't want another person to die with me."

Then, I asked her gently with tears falling down my cheeks, to end that painful call.

Breaking up with Maria Bella was another suicide for me, but this time I was obliged to obey my mind's words as the only decision left was to submit to God.

I hung up and slept as a dead creature to a late hour in the second morning.

Chapter 27

"Wondering My Life in My War's First Morning"

I opened my eyes again, checking my first morning in my mother country. I sat with my mother in the living room and couldn't stop hugging her and looking in her eyes that I had missed. I begged God for that moment again. I was still worried, but assured that my mother's health was getting better than ever.

I didn't notice that we sat more than two hours drinking coffee and talking about my days in Dubai.

My words focused on how much I missed her.

And for no reason, I asked her about the meaning of the name Maria Bella which I pretended to know randomly.

In a lovely sentence she explained the true meaning, which put a smile on my face and reminded me of the beautiful memories.

Later, I noticed that my mother was tired and dozed off.

So I moved outside quietly and walked to the same balcony that I used to stand on a year ago.

There I wondered again about solving my problems which at this time, became a result of a past decision-deserting Maria Bella- coming from a future felt vision-

Blackness- which needed to be solved through deleting everything completely from my present time.

I prayed faithfully to God to help me use my weapon, honesty, that I had received the day before.

Everything seemed okay, as I saw the neighbours sitting around and saluted them.

It was sunny and the climate was so perfect for a long stay on the balcony.

I was still afraid, but I was sure that my fears would diminish after I made sure that Mother recovered.

The view was amazing. Everyone was happy to see me again. I heard someone saying my name with a voice that I missed. It was the voice of my second mother, Elizabeth who was happy about my return.

I saluted her warmly and asked her to wait for me for a couple of minutes to visit her after changing my clothes.

Deep inside, my feelings weren't at ease. I couldn't figure out the reason. It was really confusing. I was not able to enjoy that lovely morning and it was as if I sensed that something weird was happening somewhere else. I tried to ignore this feeling by convincing myself that what my eyes were beholding was alright. It's only a fear coming from the painful past that I started to try and forget in this new day.

Thus, I looked up at the sky and thanked the Lord on that fresh start.

Again, something else shocked me.

There was still a salute missing.

The Letter M was there again, but this time without the lovely white pigeon.

I remembered what I wanted to remove from my life, and went back with my memories to the day before when I received the phone call from Maria Bella right after I asked God about her. I linked that with a similar special incident that happened in Dubai before my Term Test in 13/6 when I was on the roof.

At that time, my heart asked God for permission to love the white pigeon that he'd become addicted to.

But as usual, my mind stood obstinately in his face to stop him by saying,

"What courage are you showing?

Do you feel satisfied to betray God?

Do you want to continue doing the forbidden?

If yes, find yourself a place to hide from the Creator, or else hide from that forbidden pigeon and live peacefully everywhere."

I listened to them carefully and reminded myself by my love for the Lord and insisted on doing my best to please him.

"But what about the signs…?" my heart asked me.

"I will seek them from now on, my friend; I will consider all the signs that passed as self-punishment for my sins of disobeying God."

Then, I asked God to forgive me on everything I've done, and asked him to lead me to the right way, and to stay on the right track.

I'll do whatever it costs to stay faithful because I bled enough through my sufferings. Hence, I felt that death was my destiny.

"Help me Lord. I'm sure you will send me more signs to enlighten my way."

I said those words, but deep inside the picture of Maria Bella was what I saw.

"Yes dear", my mind said meanly while watching that image coming from my heart. "Signs will solve everything".

But suddenly, something incredible happened.

A white pigeon flew directly over my head.

I heard my heart screaming, breaking all the silence with that abrupt flight of the White Pigeon,

What do you think it is?

What on earth are you thinking of?

Haven't you noticed that it was the first white pigeon among the hundreds of coloured ones you saw in Dubai?

Haven't you also realized that it came directly after you asked God for a sign?

Or your mind was blind enough and afraid to confess that it was a sign from God. Well, I say the courage is what God ordered us to attain:

"Have I not commanded you, be strong and courageous.

Do not be afraid; do not be discouraged, for the Lord your God will be with you wherever you go." Joshua 1;9"

My heart echoed those words loudly. It was fighting in God's name.

"What should I do?" I asked my inner self. That sign made my mind confused. He kept silent astonished by the restored leader - My refreshed heart saying,

"Maybe, God's words and intentions were translated, in this moment to concrete signs. And as we know, God's words are above everything".

My notebook shall continue, but this time as it started, in the name of the Lord, I will fight with my only weapon, truthfulness, by surrendering to the Lord's will. I shall no more be the one to take the initiative in the coming events and in the war I started. I will truly wait for any response from the one who loved me. If she came back, then, let it be, and if she didn't, then let it be. Maybe like that, God wants me to be. Shall the will of God prevail.

I wrote this ending with an intention to continue my notebook in another part as an angry nun awkwardly stared at me whenever I sat in there.

I closed the book and picked up my stuff, willing to go back home because my mind warned me to behave gently with others - especially with the ones who obeyed God's words.

I tried to stand up to leave, but my legs didn't allow me to walk. The reason came from a heart who was still in the mood of writing, and asked me to continue what I started in the name God.

Well for me, and from my previous experience, I preferred trouble with that nun. It was much better than having another struggle with my inner-self.

Therefore, I avoided the idea of separating my notebook into two different parts but combine them again with the combination of my "heart" and "mind" united confronting the almighty in a lovely place.

Going back again to that balcony, I stood feverishly and wondered about the missing white pigeon, before going to Mrs. Elizabeth.

I heard the name Maria Bella from my mother, who could hardly to reach the balcony.

"What's that mother?" I asked anxiously.

"Take the phone son, a woman called Maria Bella is calling you urgently from the hospital and asking about you."

I took the phone immediately to talk with her.

But she gave me no chance to talk as she said.

"Listen to me. I don't want to disturb your life again, but I came in the early morning to the hospital for a usual check up about a simple disease I had before, but the results were negative and the doctor suggested to do the operation immediately.

And I really don't know if I would stay alive after it.

My Mother is at home with the baby and my sister needs more than two hours to come. She went to the airport to get my husband who's as usual living in his own world of business.

Please, sweetheart, I feel so lonely in this hospital. Please come and let me see you for the last time.

I need you, sweetheart.

You're the only one who could help me now.

I beg you to forget our promise just for today, and I promise that we will stop everything after I enter the operation room honey."

I said no word except,

"Hold on dear, I'll be there as soon as possible."

I quickly put on suitable clothes, I told my mother that Maria Bella was a close friend and a mother of a lovely girl who needed someone by her side before having her surgery.

Then I ran outside quickly. While closing the door, I heard my mother saying, "Do your best to help her son; I'm a mother and I know what it means to face death.

I will be praying for her. Just move quickly. May the Lord bless her and get her back to her family."

I took my sports motorcycle which I hadn't driven for long, but chose to take it to avoid traffic congestion.

I felt protected after hearing my mother's prayers for my pure intention of helping a mother survive and have a new life, as I wanted before.

I rode it fast and arrived to the hospital in a short time.

When I reached the door of her room, I saw the doctor standing. He was worried about her case. He was asking for blood donors to be able to do the operation.

I approached him and asked about her. He answered by asking me to quickly find anyone of the same rare blood group to start the operation immediately or death would be her fate.

I finished that quick conversation and dashed into the room to see the one who made my heart beat again.

"Why didn't you tell me before?" I asked her sadly.
"I wanted to tell you my little secret, but your promise made it meaningless." She answered sadly.

"You didn't even say a word for a year, Maria Bella." I blamed her.
"I think you are the only person who feels and knows why we hide our sickness," she said with tears in her eyes then continued,
"You were my only hope in my dark moments.
I was so afraid before you came. I thought I will never see you again.
I don't know what anything means to me except having you beside me.
But thank God that you returned.
You came in the perfect time before God takes my soul.
It's really the best happy ending, sweetheart."

"Stop those words, Maria Bella," I interrupted toughly.
"You're going to live again. You will have a new life better than the one we had together," I said with tears falling down my cheeks.

"Please, don't feel sorry for me. I deserve more than death. Maybe, I wasn't truthful with God in my past decisions, but now I've learned so much from you, and I'm convinced about my condition."

You really helped me know what it means to abide by God's words and to make it priority in my life.

The last thing the doctor said is that I need blood and he still couldn't find any donor. This means that I will die within the hands of someone truthful like you, sweetheart.

I think it's the best ending; exactly the same I dreamt about a long time ago."

I hushed to her toughly.

"You will be fine, Maria Bella, just stop talking like that. The Doctor found a blood donor and the operation will be smoother and easier than you think."

"Who told you that?" She asked me then said,

"I heard the Doctor secretly telling the nurse before he left a while ago."

I answered in a soft voice, "I heard him telling the nurse that blood units for donation are ready directly before I entered.

So please, don't be depressed and let me freely ask you my last request, Maria Bella."

She kept silent as if it was the first time she listened to my words in a way of acceptance of the Lord's will as a new promise.

"You will live, sweetie.

You will have a new peaceful life again

But before, you must promise me to forget the love that you gave for me. We were not born for each other, Maria Bella.

You are married, and you have a sweet girl.

And I repeat that even if you were single, I'm a sick person who can't do anything besides except preparing himself to face God.

I want you to change the love you gave for me with a brotherly affection and feelings to keep away as forbidden memories.

We will not follow or even ask about each other after you open your eyes again from this surgery.

I beg you to forget everything and to remember me as a brother.

Just promise me now and I am sure that God will forgive us our sins and he will bring you back to life with a new essence."

She didn't say any word, as if she preferred death to applying this promise.

"Don't ignore the Lord's way.

It's your only way to survive."

I said my words and took off my bracelet which she was still looking at, then put it in her hand.

"I think this moment is the perfect one for you to be again truthful with God." I said that with a pure intention to a dear sister.

Her continuous silence made me press on her arms and repeat nervously, "Promise me now, Maria Bella".

She was weak before my honest request, which gave her no choice but to accept the Lord's Will, by saying,

"I promise you sweetheart."

Thank God that I had her promise before the nurse entered and directly injected the anaesthesia to start the operation, then said loudly,

"The surgery will start within minutes, please sir go to the donation room and I will come back to you."

I tried to avoid Maria Bella's eyes but couldn't stop her slow words,

"What are you doing?

This is craziness.

You will kill yourself.

Please don't.

I don't want to do the operation", she uttered these words with a sleepy voice.

I hugged her quickly, in a way not to let the nurse hear her words. Then gave my soul mate sister a head goodbye kiss while she was losing her consciousness.

I went to the donation room to give out blood. The nurse obviously believed me that I was sickness free. I was of the same blood group with Maria Bella.

The nurse inserted a sterilized needle, she waited for my blood to fill the bag.

I remained silent and asked My Lord to complete this mission safely.

I laid my head on the bench and listened to my inner words again.

"My Lord, my Lord, my Lord", I heard from my mind praying as ordering all my senses to stay tuned. My heart obeyed his words as a last order and cooperated with no objection. Maybe because it was the only choice to stay alive.

Or, maybe, they both had one desire, had one intention, and had a belief that God is the only one who could make a miracle and save them if they were both truly seeking him.

"My Lord", was what I repeated with a tired smile on the bench as my pressure started to increase when the nurse took off the needle from my vein.

I was relieved that blood was secured for my soul mate.

The door was closed, and my pressure kept increasing. My heartbeats were strongly felt. My eyes and veins almost popped.

Everything around me became black.

I recognized well that I was losing my consciousness.

My voice was mute, all my body became paralyzed.

What was happening was a dream, a dream where I was only allowed to count my breaths.

That black image took me to the image of Dr. Sam's black glasses, and as if my mind allowed that memory to come just to remind me of my failure in my spiritual duties and so to ask God more for forgiveness.

My hope to survive became null and counting my breaths started to fade away.

"My Lord, my Lord, my Lord," was repeated.

I tried to figure out that new raising voice. "My Lord, my Lord, my Lord", was repeated louder.

But this time by another voice.

By a voice who screamed loudly with confidence that he succeeded through my duties.

That voice had its peak when a bright creature appeared so close to my eyes.

It was that white pigeon stained scarlet but flying powerfully as if it was thanking me with the letter M- our initials- formed in the arrangement of her surrounding pigeons.

"My Lord, my Lord, my Lord", I was ending this image, even though the feeling of drowsiness became totally dominating. My smile came again when I discovered that this voice was truly said by my 'heart' who became one with my mind under the name of God.

"He is awake, yes finally he is fine. He came back good.

Hey crazy wake up, wake up our crazy hero.

You could have put us and yourself in trouble.

Thank God that everything went fine. You must have been dead for what you did.

I think your mother should punish you on that.

Just wake up and go tell her about your craziness.

You made us all really worried about you."

Was what I heard from the doctor surrounded by my brother and many nurses who were checking the biological signs.

"How is she?
Has she survived the surgery?"
I asked the Doctor slowly.

"She asked the same question about you, yesterday before she went home. Your blood came perfectly on time. She must never forget about your nobility.

But, we told her that you are okay and you will also be home as soon as you recover fully."

Chapter 28

"New Life with Old Shadows"

Even if I didn't intend to disclose my little secret, I came home and knew that everyone around had officially known about my sickness.

"It's my fault son, I was the reason of your misery, I should have taken care of you," My mother blamed herself for leaving me when I was weak.

"I should have listened to you when we were speaking before you travelled.

Forgive me son for being tough with you. I should have been a better mother."

"Stop that mother," I interrupted, but she continued.

"Thank God that he got you back to me. I would have killed myself if something happened to you." I tried my best to convince her that I was fine and had a new experience abroad, but my words were meaningless with her feeling of guilt.

Everything was getting better; I felt good while surrounded by the warmth of family.

I continued working in the domain of teaching, but in my country.

I became a mathematics teacher again, but for secondary levels at a charity school near my village.

Though, I had a smaller salary compared to the one in Dubai, working comfortably with an administration was what I needed to have self-esteem and for my work to be appreciated. They were glad to have me in their team unified in one spirit with good surroundings who brought up a good generation.

I loved the idea of teaching especially when I bonded with my adult students and taught them how to avoid sins through their daily behaviour with people who aren't meant to be for us.

(My smile appeared again but this time, it was really for my students not for someone else).

For no reason, I got afraid many times, but with a strong will, I tried to get over my fears by trying to cling to my promise and stopped any single idea which could remind me of Maria Bella.

I even refrained from looking to the sky and gave no interest to any sign I saw.

Being truthful to the words of God became the secret of my happiness.

I was impressed by my mind who had a strong control to delete all the memories that were not suitable and not right to me.

But surely, the deleting process was done by the permission of my heart who finally became convinced to have the Lord as his only master.

He impressed me too by his new attitude that showed me the feelings of a brother, in time he passed on the memory of a girl that had once his bracelet- charm.

Finally, I lived the peace that I was craving for before in my country and with the people who got adapted to my new peaceful reality.

I recovered well, and took advantage to practice martial arts; secretly that was an addiction in my whole life.

I thanked the Lord profoundly for his fatherly warmth that I sensed among all the people around me.

Accepting the Lord's will was not easy, but was finally achieved after that good and bitter experience I went through.

Days passed quickly and I sat always beside the grave of my dear Robert, putting some flowers in the fifth of every month.

I perfectly understood that everything happens is a test as Mr. Sam said. I wanted to sit with him, but I wasn't courageous enough to face him again.

I felt shameful to go his apartment without wearing his sacred bracelet- charm.

Instead, I have always prayed for my Lord and asked him to forgive me on the way I behaved with Sam then I tried daily to apply his words which were my secret treasure.

I was totally convinced that everything happens for a reason.

The traveling decision that I took previously was inevitable to submit to the Lord's will by living again as an honest person in my country.

Also, I accepted Robina's engagement to a lovely and mature person who insisted on a quick marriage after he showed her loyalty and love way better than my previous selfishness.

All the events proved to me that the one who owns the world puts every person in his right position.

Even though, there were some missing parts in my response to some disturbing events, but I was really happy again while recalling the Greatness of my Lord that I strongly believed in.

My friends visited me after, and lived again what we missed when I was away. Within those times, I was disturbed when they spoke about the victories against my previous opponent who became undefeated after he competed with me.

That idea was the only stressing one left after I lived in peace again. It made me to practice continuously to face him again and to break his incredible results.

It was dangerous to participate in championships again, but on the other hand, it was an awful memory that I was unable to delete from my history.

I went to the university and told them that I wanted to participate in the Thai-boxing championship which was held on the 3rd of May of that year. The coach wasn't sure about my readiness and asked me if my health was good enough to fight.

I told the coach to end the match if I lasted to the second round and I felt dizzy. I told him that I would try to end the match from the first round by a knock out. I didn't care for the consequences as much as I cared for defeating that stubborn opponent.

There were still two days for the Championship and all my friends were surprised to know about my registration in the competition.

Chapter 29

"The Secret Harbinger"

I was walking in my village and gladly talking with a friend I used to know in Dubai.

We passed by an old empty house. We were curious and dared to enter it slowly. My friend continued his talks, as I listened only. I kept silent noticing the antiques which looked dusty.

A music box attracted me and I tried to open it smoothly. Suddenly, my friend disappeared and a bright light came out of that box.

I was confused. My feelings got touched and wanted to scream since it reminded me of someone I missed a lot.

"You will win sweetheart; this time, you will truly win."

I saw someone glowing beside me and said those words softly.

My heartbeats raced as a response. I was so emotionally touched to a level I started to breathe heavily and longed to see the person I sincerely missed. It was Maria Bella.

"I thought I would never see you again. What are you doing in this empty house?"

"Just tell me about you, Maria Bella." I fondly asked her.

"I'm here to tell you about your new life dear.

It will start from tomorrow. You will win the championship and will live strong forever." She said with a shining smile.

"Are you going to be with the spectators? I asked happily. But she kept silent.

"I'm asking you, why don't you answer?" I asked feverishly.

But as if she didn't want to spoil my happy moments, she answered gently but sadly.

"I don't want to increase my bill."

What bill? I asked nervously again.

But she suddenly held a large golden cross and interrupted my words by kissing it, then softly uttered,

"You were my bill and I was your test sweetheart.

The coming days will prove those words for you."

But her sacred gesture with the cross and her words couldn't stop me from shouting toughly.

"I do not understand your words. Just answer my question. Are you going to come to the match tomorrow?"

But with the same crying eyes and with a descending voice, she answered,

"I want to stay alone, but I repeat that tomorrow, you will win sweetheart.

Don't forget that I was your test as you were my bill."

"Maria Bella, what's going on?

Why are you saying these words?

Answer me, Maria Bella.

Maria Bella... Maria Bella."

It was a dream.

I woke up echoing her name and crying as never before.

I couldn't imagine that I was still in love with this lady that much. Her words were digging deep inside my heart. I couldn't believe that it was a dream. I looked around to check if I was able to see her in my room.

I picked up my phone and called her without caring for my promise or even for her husband.

It was almost dawn, and calling her at that time could subject her to troubles with her husband. But I couldn't think logically because I craved to hear her voice. I braved all the boldness and called while I looked out from the window but in vain. I couldn't; her number was unavailable.

"It means she was better than I was and dumped her number to keep our promise," was what I thought about that action.

I headed to the university the day before the championship. Unexpectedly, I noticed just before entering the ring quarter, that even the lovely tree that was in the middle of the campus and on which the initials of my name and Robina's was cut down and the decoration of the university was all changed as if all the past was removed.

I saw the coach and told him again about my plan in giving my opponent a quick knockout from the first round, in order to avoid the second round.

Then I insisted to stay tuned to my moves in case I continued playing to the second round. I asked him to throw the white towel if he saw me losing control.

My coach hesitated, and advised me again not to enter the ring, but my long thirst for victory gave him no chance to argue because I was responsible for myself.

I looked at the audience expecting to see Maria Bella. But anyway, that dream I had was so real and gave me the courage to fight for my soul mate sister who appeared this time to be cheering for the crazy person instead of the opponent who represented her university.

I entered the match and gave my best. My consecutive hits were fast enough to have control over my opponent.

But he was sharply trained and had the chance to go to the second round.

My coach was worried and asked me if I can continue.

I kept silent and waited for the last moments of the second round to give the chance for the knockout to answer that question.

I heard the audience cheering for me because I won the match. I was very active and ready to play another two matches. I couldn't believe that I was so fit. I went down the ring and asked my audience to forgive me for not attending the second match.

My heart beat normally even while running quickly to the parking lot.

I drove to the same hospital for a full check up again for my health.

I looked at the monitor that was checking my heart for signs of weakness. It was the moment of truth which a poor dreamer had dreamt about.

It was so similar to a great dream coming true. It was a miracle and something totally unexpected.

"It seems your heart lied to you previously, or else God's hand has touched you, son," was what the doctor said.

"It's a miracle!" was what I heard from my doctor. "Your health is perfect. It seems you are loved by the Lord, son" the doctor repeated.

"I think now you can go and tell everybody about your health, it's perfect.

I'm sure your mother never stopped praying for you," he continued.

It was definitely a miracle.

Those words made me want to fly on clouds. It was more than a human mind can imagine.

I called my mother and told her that I was totally cured.

I came down the streets and started to run as fast as I could.

I drove back home and sat with my family. All were astonished, and thanked God for his mercy.

I tried to call Maria Bella again to tell her about everything.

But again, her phone was out of reach.

I also tried to call Mr. Sam, but the same happened, his phone was out of reach.

I ran down Mrs. Elizabeth's home and told her that the eagle which we spoke about previously was back with stronger wings and he is soaring again high in the sky.

I asked her about Mr. Sam, but she answered, "He left his village to a far place eight months ago without any details about his whereabouts. But before leaving, he came to say goodbye and asked about you, then said that he was searching for some people who decided to be truthful. But later, and after he finds them, he will leave the country to a place where he can spend his time worshipping God."

Chapter 30

"Objecting Destiny"

It was still afternoon. I asked Elizabeth to excuse me for a while to leave with a promise to come back later, then took my motorcycle and drove to the top of the mountain. There, I stood with myself with the pure intention to check on someone else.

I called my previous friends in Dubai and asked them about Maria Bella. I was thrilled to talk with her. But no one knew anything. They all said that she left the school at the same time when I did.

Even she didn't contact anyone from her close friends.

Those answers made me feel worried about that white swan. I sat on the ground and looked at the sky, then asked God to give me the courage to call her husband's company. I only cared to know about Maria Bella. But that company was a big one and her husband was a famous manager. I stood up and called with a different name, then asked the operator to connect me with him.

"Sorry sir, but Mr. Antony left the company from around eleven months ago. We are sorry to tell you that he had a terrible car accident with his family and left us forever.

We are so sorry to tell you also that we have no connections with any of his relatives.

May God rest their souls in peace."

My legs shook and shivered roughly while hearing those words.

"My Lord.

My Lord.

My Lord." I screamed.

"What has she done to deserve that fate?

What have you made with her?

She was a good person. She believed in you and tried to apply your words in her life.

She is an innocent person and she doesn't deserve death.

My Lord!" I shouted again.

"Why have you commanded her soul?

Why did you introduce her to me?

She was killed twice.

I killed her first when you brought me to her life, then you killed her another time when she truly found you in her life.

I've done what you said, and we both obeyed your words. She truthfully promised as I also did to follow your path.

This is unfair.

It is all unfair, My Lord.

My Lord, my Lord, my Lord"

I cried loudly and screamed those sentences after that horrible call. I shrieked deep inside and ran to the woods aimlessly.

All the tough acts I've done with her flashed before my eyes.

She used to feel that death was close and tried to have some happiness before she left, but it was not meant for her.

I lay on the ground and tried to gain control by taking a deep breath. Then tried to convince myself that it was the Lord's will, but in vain.

My tears ran down heavily.

It was the hardest moment I ever faced.

I couldn't imagine a trial that could reach the level to accept the Lords will via the death of a person who became finally my soul mate sister, and whom I wanted to thank deeply for saving me from my own self.

I kept crying for more than two hours, then came back home and slept all night and the whole day after.

My heart was shredded.

My happiness was totally turned off after that call.

I couldn't eat for twenty-four hours.

I told my Mom about Maria Bella and asked to pray for her soul and the soul of her family.

After, I couldn't stay at home, and as usual, I went to my neighbour Mrs. Elizabeth who was the source of my inspiration.

I sat and told her again everything. I confessed to her my objection to the Lord's will and showed that the coming of the strong eagle was meaningless after he lost the passion to fly again.

"Do you think Maria Bella is hearing you, now?" Mrs. Elizabeth asked in a way that showed she understood again my pain.

I understood the spiritual level of her question, and tried to answer her by what I saw in my dream that was real for me.

"I'm pretty sure of that. She appeared alive in my dream and foretold me everything I experience even into the incidents occurred in the past days. .

Her words were exactly translated into reality. I'm sure that her soul is with me and was the one who saved me from my sickness," I answered.

But in this very moment, Mrs. Elizabeth, as usual, advised me.

"Go sit with her in a place that means a lot to you, and write for her all your feelings. I'm sure that she will hear you better; maybe she wants to listen for those words alone with you.

Write for her in the same intention you both promised after you gave her my lovely bracelet." She said, with a smile that changed my mood.

Then she continued, "Let your inner-self show her how eagles love with nobility, innocence and loyalty unlike all other creatures, but surely, under the name of God."

Mrs. Elizabeth was incredible; she drove me to find a way to smile back at every time I thought it was doom day.

Chapter31

"Facing Destiny"

I went back home and took a lovely notebook, then went to a church in which Maria Bella chose to have her marriage.

It was in a place far from my home, but I didn't care for the distance as much as I cared for the place from where I begot tranquillity in the presence of God Almighty.

It was one of the best places I ever visited.

I walked in as if I was with her. It was déjà vu. I imagined I was there before recollecting her memories when she vowed to apply God's words before she met me.

I chose to sit on a lovely bench in the garden of that grotesque church which was surrounded by trees.

I could feel the breeze stroking my hands as my confidence heightened when my "inner" was finally led by my "heart" and my "mind" simultaneously under the name of God.

Then I truly asked the Lord to give me the power to write my notebook to commemorate her memory forever and show her the pain I went through to walk in the shade of God's path.

The first memory which came to mind was when I asked her to break up with me in the worst morning I ever had before leaving Dubai.

In that day, we both left school shell-shocked about that decision.

She couldn't believe what I said, and couldn't stay home. She told her husband that she wanted to go outdoors to bring some stuff for the flight, but in reality, she was trying to go anywhere just to get some time on her own and think of what had happened.

My feelings were the same, and I also went outdoors in a friend's car for the same reason.

Nothing ran down my brain except a song which we both loved.

I called the radio station and asked the operator to play "Broken Angel" a song which we both considered the best to describe our real story. I wished my Lord to accept this song as a final gift dedicated for Maria Bella.

And by coincidence, the woman who used only to use the CDs in her car turned on the radio at this time.

I received a call from Maria Bella to tell me that fate chose her that we listen to our song at the goodbye moments.

My strong belief in that memory reassured me that Maria Bella's soul will definitely read my Notebook as a true and final gift. I indeed started writing my Notebook on May 5th around a year after she passed.

Back then, I had been writing my book for many days. I remember, I daily wrote for minimum three hours non-stop till sunset.

It was the best days of my life. I lived a spiritual connection with someone I truly loved. Writing in God's holy place gave me a sense of satisfaction and peace of mind.

I couldn't ignore the disturbance I had from the nun who used to look weirdly at me after my recurrent sitting on that lovely bench.

But I cared less for residing in a wonderful peaceful world and it was enough to forget my trivial through.

I finished the book, and I wanted to keep on writing.

I checked it carefully so as not to have anything missing. It was something I thanked God for achieving.

Maria Bella's last gift could finally be ready if it weren't for one missing thing- the title.

I was really confused about the title.

"Peace in Wars of Love", was the name I wanted to use as a title for this book. I saw it perfectly describing the story inside, but "A Memory to Remember", was another title that showed the same meaning.

I was confused, but both were of the same percentage.

And so, I chose to keep My Notebook with no title to leave it for Maria Bella's soul to put the title by her own for an inner war with myself done to feed her in her new path by showing my credibility and attachment to God's words and commandments.

I flipped the pages to the cover and confidently kept "My Notebook" empty, just as white as my intention to her lovely pure white soul.

I looked around in the holy place and admitted that the book was written indeed only by the will of the Lord.

I went to the annoyed nun again and asked her to bear with me for one more day, because the day after will be my last day to come to this lovely church because I want to photocopy my book.

The nun was at ease after hearing my unexpected request and went inside the church to tell another nun about my perfect step.

I felt glad to avoid any trouble with those respectful nuns. I went away leaving all my past in that lovely book to start again a new and a fresh life.

I came back home happily and told everyone about my comfort after writing this book which had changed my life.

Surely, Mrs. Elizabeth was the first to know; she was proud at her little eagle who was soaring higher than ever on its proper course.

I made the second copy and went back to that church to see the same nun who was interested about my idea of leaving, waiting for me beside my lovely bench.
"I just wonder if you could give my book to the abbess and to put it in a safe place for someone gone to read." I said.
"She will surely accept if you really leave this bench," she smiled sarcastically while saying those words.

I pretended that I didn't notice her previous disturbance and asked why.

"This bench is the main place for all the nuns to pray every evening Sir," she said again strictly.
"I'm really sorry, please forgive me, dear, but why you didn't tell me?
I could have chosen another bench in that peaceful church."
I said with a true feeling of guilt.
"The abbess had the feeling that you are honest and didn't allow any of us to disturb you. For twenty one days, she had been watching you from her room facing the bench

seriously writing that book." The nun answered as if she was blaming the abbess on her decision.

"Can I meet her?
Please, I really want to apologize for my selfish behaviour." I said again.

"I'm sorry to tell you that she can't meet anyone for the time being for she is the newly assigned Abbess in our monastery, and chose to dedicate her first months in worshipping God.

But she gave me a special gift for you." She murmured.

"Oh please, I don't deserve all this kindness," I commented while waiting, with no reason to see what the nun hid in her pocket.

"It's her own sacred-bracelet", she said as she picked a lovely wooden bracelet from her pocket.

Then continued,

"This bracelet had never left her hand, and as everyone here knows, that it saved her twice from death.

First time, from a dangerous surgery around a year ago, and the second time when she lost all her family including her daughter, mother, husband and sister in a car, while she was spared. She only received bruises while wearing this bracelet.

It ... really is a mystery. She received it from a truthful person who was given it buy another truthful person.

But what we all wanted to know was the bracelet's first owner.

He was an aged and white old man with dark glasses. He came to this church previously and convinced us all to elect the current nun a new abbess after the death of the former one.

He said that this bracelet should be worn by honest people only.

We were all surprised to have that young lady as our superior .But later, her attitude showed that she was a very humble and experienced believer.

Soon, she gained our love and respect for her ultimate dedication to the words of God. I'm sure that this bracelet will make a difference in your life. You're blessed by our abbess who chose to give it for you."

I couldn't believe the nun's words, but as soon as the bracelet was returned to me I smiled, and felt again the peace of mind I had so desperately craved.

I asked the nun to give me my notebook back, picked up my pen again and finally wrote a title which represented the truth of my story, , "Twenty One Days".

The nun was impressed and said that her abbess was not mistaken to give a talented writer her best bracelet. Then, she asked me directly about my secret of writing a book in such a short time.

I didn't say anything. I kept silent for a moment and looked back to the bracelet in my hand, then answered by writing these words on the book's cover below the title,

"It all comes down to how truthful we are."

Then she responded with a forgiving smile; to which I smiled back. Deep inside I knew my smile was meant for another girl - the girl who became my sister, and was surely grinning up in her building facing the bench.

"Please be sure to give this book for your abbess as a goodbye gift from me and to apologize for my disturbance before leaving this church forever" I said with a true goodbye smile. I looked towards the wooden shaded window with all respect in front of the nun.

After this, I stayed silent and walked happily away from that church, looking at the letters M & H printed on my lovely bracelet.

My best memories ended after leaving that church, but they (my memories) were smart enough to choose the ending in the same place, where they started.

Standing again on the balcony of my home I noticed clearly the Letter M through the arrangement of the flying pigeons, with a lovely white one shining brightly. This time I was overwhelmed with vigorous passion to experience fresh and new memories of a promising future yet to come- a future built on a lovely yet complicated past that was now cleaned and purified in the present time without confusion. My mind's perception of the daily visions sent from the master of my heart- the heart who finally applied the words of God- shall be my driving force to be faithful and truthful forever.

"Ending"

I remember saying: "I write life and others read it", before writing my first official book. I also recall the impressive words that Maria Bella's Grandmother used to say:
"We are always enemies of the unknown."

Well, I concluded that ending my best memories with these two sayings was done for a reason.

Honestly, after I finished writing my notebook "Twenty One days", I discovered that everyone in the world has their own Notebook.
But unfortunately, we all become enemies of our own selves when we connect our writings personally, whereas in reality we are mere readers of our own pre-written stories published only by the Real Writer known unanimously as The Lord, Almighty.

Proverbs:

When you talk the best words with an intention of goodness, then you are like the listener, learning to feel what you are repeating.

M.H.
Mohannad.Halaby

Humans learn to love their enemies when they discover the real enemy inside themselves.

M.H.
Mohannad.Halaby

Never do we have to face the world but just ourselves.

M.H.
Mohannad.Halaby

We fall by our acts for a wisdom to rise as believers.

M.H.
Mohannad.Halaby